DESIGNING YOUR IDEAL LIFE

CREATE YOUR BLUEPRINT FOR SUCCESS AND HAPPINESS

BECKY LYNN SMITH

Ideal Life
Publishing

Published by:

Ideal Life Publishing

12138 County Road 314

Navasota, TX 77868

In Partnership with:

A Book's Mind

PO Box 272847

Fort Collins, CO 80527

www.abooksmind.com

Copyright © 2015 Becky Lynn Smith

ISBN: 978-1-939828-19-4

Library of Congress Control Number: 2014954457

Printed in the United States of America

CONTENTS

FOREWORD – ROGER WRIGHT

In this book, Becky Lynn Smith recalls a message from Don Clifton, a positive psychology pioneer:

Everybody does one thing better than ten thousand other people.

That's the good news.

The bad news?

Most of us have no idea what that one thing is.

What is that "one thing" for you? Even more important, how does that "one thing" fit into the full, vibrant, and fulfilling life you seek? Everyone's answer will of course be different. And what's so exciting for every one of us is that in *Designing Your Ideal Life*, Ms. Smith charts a path and gives each one of us the tools to succeed.

I used to work for The Gallup Organization — Mr. Clifton's company. As you probably know, Gallup collects data and studies almost everything from elections to workplace engagement and anything in between.

One question that has been asked for decades is "At work I get to do what I do best every day." Sadly only 20 percent of us by our own admission say yes to that question. Which means that at least 80 percent of us are just going through the motions. Doing stuff to get paid.

But what if those numbers were transposed and most of us were able to go to work every day and do something we love? What impact would that have on our world, our families, productivity or even our *Ideal Life?* Interested in the answer? Then you will be interested in this book.

We all have hints about what we are good at, what we would LOVE doing every day. When you were a kid, what were you drawn to? Numbers? Words? Building things? Saying things? Were you kinetic and constantly moving or were you able to sit for hours and solve one problem? As we grow older we somehow suppress all of that so called 'childish' stuff, and we get a little lost in the muddle of moving forward, making a paycheck, reaching for the next role or rung on the ladder.

I have been there. I know how difficult it is to reassess where you are when you should be counting your blessings. Or at least counting your dollars. Your so called 'success' creates momentum, and it's hard not to lose yourself in all of the accolades and the security that comes with doing something that provides a regular paycheck.

But, we only have one life. This one. The one we are in right now. One chance to use our gifts and talents to make a difference in the world — THE difference that we are intended to make. If you are there and you are in the 20 percent of people doing what you do best every day, then count your blessings, name them one by one, and keep going.

And, if you are in that group that hasn't figured out what your ONE THING is, then take heart. There are many of us who have been right there, and who know how difficult it is. If you've picked up a copy of Becky Lynn Smith's *Designing Your Ideal Life*, you must be pretty sure that you are not living your ideal life, the one that God intended for you to live. You've taken a big step, because this book and its ideas will challenge your status quo and make you even more uncomfortable as you get off the moving train you have been on and readjust your life and your goals.

Ms. Smith will ask you to get in touch with your dreams again, to revisit your childhood inclinations, long buried under the years of work and time and the cares of this life that we all deal with on a daily basis. She'll give you a roadmap and checkpoints along the way to figure out where you should be. She will tell you that she, too, has been there in the corner office but still unable to shake that gnawing feeling that there was more for her.

Indeed there was. After a few fits and starts, she has found the one thing she was meant to do. And, her first thought upon discovering her life's work was to help others find theirs. This book and the companion workbook will do just that.

Hopefully you'll find your calling and get to work on something you love. And, I'll tell you this: Working on something you love is not really work at all. Though it's not always easy, there is a joy in doing what you love. And, because it comes from your soul, you think about it a lot, you are constantly rehearsing how to do it better, and you can't wait to get to work every day.

I know something about this because I, too, have finally found my calling. I've always been a writer at heart. And, for many years I did other things that I was pretty good at — consulting, managing people, climbing up and up the corporate ladder. Then, one day, it hit me with an embarrassing simplicity. "I'm a writer! Why aren't I writing?"

I started my journey with baby steps. I began to write a blog under the banner of Salon.com. The writing got better on a curated blog called fictionique.com. And, then a few years ago I co-authored a book called *I Am Your Neighbor: Voices From a Chicago Food Pantry*. Writing in the spirit of a personal hero, Studs Terkel. And helping to build a financial future for an organization that fed hungry people? It was, just like Ms. Smith said the beginning of, "an ideal life."

So, I wrote another book. *Finding Work When There Are No Jobs*. A way of thinking differently about finding work. A way that very much follows the path you are about to take here. I was written up in Forbes. I became a regular contributor to The Huffington Post. I hear from people all over the country who have read my books. They tell me the difference they have made in their lives, and every part of it all is priceless.

In short, I am in Heaven. And it seemed so out of reach only a few years ago. The secret? Being willing to stop and examine my strengths and abilities and talents and be honest about who I really am, and then act upon it. It was as scary as anything I have ever done, and yet today I find myself in the place that I was somehow always intended to be.

Great things happen when we discover that one thing we do better than ten thousand others. Once we embark on that journey, the potential for real impact and excellence grows exponentially.

Like it could grow for you.

So, congratulations. Your life is about to change because you, in your heart of hearts, know there is more and you are brave enough to admit it. My advice?

Don't just read this book. Use it! Answer the questions. Your answers will be the foundation for designing your ideal life.

No one else's ideal life.

Just yours.

ACKNOWLEDGEMENTS

I am blessed with amazing family and friends. I would like to thank you for your encouragement and support. I would like to extend a very special *thank you* to Dennis Welch, who believed in me and offered his encouragement to complete this book, and to Craig Carter who told me he would actually buy it.

I would also like to acknowledge those who taught me much about life, but may not have known it. My parents and stepparents, my son, Jason, my best friend, Norma, my stepsister, Cindalynn, my friend, Sue Muzzy, and many others too numerous to name. You have blessed me beyond what I deserve. I am grateful.

CHAPTER ONE: INTRODUCTION

INTRODUCTION

Our prime purpose in this life is to help others. And if you can't help them, at least don't hurt them. — Dalai Lama

Life is short. Many people blindly go through the motions of living, but are not happy and don't know why. You only have to look around at the people, who seemingly have everything going for them, to realize that they are not happy either. Movie stars, athletes, musicians – we are surrounded by talented people who have money and fame and are still miserable. The people who drown their emotions with alcohol, drugs, food, sex, or other addictions, are clearly trying to escape from something. What are they missing? Why are they unhappy? Perhaps you are also struggling.

As a society, we have our priorities backward. We get so wrapped up in the day-to-day turmoil that we forget our true purpose in life is to make a difference in the lives of others. It often takes a life-changing event for us to realize we need to make a change. Perhaps you picked up this book because you realize you also need a change. I believe that only by making a difference in the lives of others can we experience the true joy of living.

Happiness is not an accident. Nor is it something you wish for. Happiness is something you design. — Jim Rohn

The premise of this book is simple. The path to happiness begins with your decision to be happy. Simple really, yet as most of us go through the motions we forget what it takes to be happy. In fact, happiness is not that simple. Happiness starts with the desire to intentionally create a life of purpose—a life in which we choose to make a difference in the world.

Creating a happy life is not a destination, but a process. The objective of this book is to provide you with the steps required to design your ideal life. You will find a process you can follow to create your personal blueprint for success and happiness. Be sure and go to our website at DesigningYourIdealLife.com and sign up to download the companion workbook. To find the access code, flip to Chapter Nine and look under the **Tools of Self Discovery**. Reading the book, and actively participating by working the exercises, will be a first step toward taking action to create your blueprint for success and happiness. It will help you gain the clarity and focus you need to take action. Please feel free to send your feedback, or drop a line and let me know if the book was helpful—or to offer your suggestions for improvement. My purpose in writing it is to help you create your ideal life of happiness and abundance. Now...on to your future.

MY JOURNEY

Your purpose in life is to find your purpose and give your whole heart and soul to it. — Guatama Buddha

Success is the trap that keeps many people from finding their true purpose and happiness. For years, I believed that success included achieving the next rung on the corporate ladder. Yet, I also had a nagging feeling that I just did not fit into the corporate mold. I had all the trappings of success. I made good money. I had a title and a corner office. Yet, I was still not happy. I had climbed the corporate ladder, but did not find the happiness I thought would be at the top. Success became the trap that kept me from pursuing my true purpose and happiness. Maybe this rings true for you. The solution for me was to reinvent myself to find purpose and happiness. Perhaps my story and the tools found in this book and on the companion website will inspire you to know that success and happiness are possible for you. You have the power to live the ideal life you desire.

My reinvention started after my divorce in 1987, at the age of 30. I had a small child to support, and I knew I would not get financial help from his father. I needed to be a better provider, so I enrolled at Texas Tech University and attended school full-time while continuing to work at a bank. I completed my degree in three years with a 4.0 GPA. After graduating, I was hired as a systems analyst for a major oil company in Houston. In 1998, I received my MBA from the University of Houston. I climbed the corporate ladder through a series of strategic job changes and successful projects. I was making more money than I had ever made in my life. I was the epitome of success—or so it seemed.

Fast-forward ten years. A series of defining moments led to the discovery that I was living my life in the wrong order. The first defining moment was when my stepsister, who was my age, died of a brain tumor. I began to evaluate the meaning and purpose of my own life. Although I had achieved the level of success that I had strived for in my career, I began to feel that my job existed just to make the company's owners richer. Actions taken toward employees by the company's senior executives confirmed this feeling. I was miserable, and I felt guilty about being so unhappy. I had it all, right? I should have been happy—but I wasn't. I started searching for other options. What I realized was I did not really want another job. I wanted and needed something more.

The meaning of life is to find your gift. The purpose of life is to give it away. — Pablo Picasso

The next defining moment came when I left my corporate job to purchase a business-coaching franchise. I found joy in helping small business owners. I formed strong connections with the entrepreneurs, professionals, and business owners who were passionate about their purpose. I believed in their dream, and I wanted to help them succeed. This is the secret of a strong purpose: people will line up to help you when they believe in your cause. Articulating a worthwhile purpose will energize you and inspire others to join you on your mission.

After leaving a comfortable corporate job, I struggled as a new business owner and coach. Although I loved helping business owners and their teams, I hated chasing people for money. As a result of my limiting beliefs, my business and personal finances suffered. After my personal savings ran out, I had to make a tough decision. After much soul searching, I decided to give up my coaching franchise. I started the painful process of notifying my clients about my decision, while honoring the commitments I had made. Some might consider this a failure, but I have no regrets about the experience. I gained many client friendships and an increased personal awareness. I discovered that I am happiest when I am helping other people achieve their dreams through my writing, speaking, and teaching. I quickly found a new job to support my family. I was once again making a solid living, but I was not making the difference I wanted to make. I really felt that I should be doing more to help others.

We all have two choices: We can make a living or we can design a life. — *Jim Rohn*

The last defining moment hit me one day driving home from a good friend's funeral. I realized that most of us have our priorities backward. We are so focused on making a living, like I had been, that we miss out on opportunities for happiness. True happiness comes when we focus first on making a difference for others, followed closely by making a life by spending time with the important people in our lives. When we are able to make our living by serving others, we will find success and happiness.

Learn to be happy with what you have while you pursue all that you want. — *Jim Rohn*

I have learned through my journey that true happiness comes from living for a purpose. What we focus on makes all the difference. I believe that happiness is not found in a job, or a title, or money. **Happiness is found in the belief that you are making a difference in the world for others, including your loved ones**. You can start where you are today to create the life you want to live. If you are working at a job that does not bring you joy, look for ways to bring your life into alignment. Take small steps everyday to get there.

My share is to do the work. God's share is to give me the heart, courage and determination to do it. — Where the Red Fern Grows

My purpose in writing this book is to help you create the blueprint for your ideal life of success and happiness. I am truly blessed to be able to make a difference in the lives of others. In so doing, I am making a positive difference in my own life and in the lives of my loved ones. You have the ability to do the same. Just start where you are today. You can make a life AND make a living. Life is way too short to spend it being unhappy. Choose happiness.

YOU ARE WORTHY

Before we get started, please do this one thing for me. It sounds like a crazy request, but please humor me for just one minute. Are you ready? Please take this book into your bedroom or bathroom—wherever you have a mirror you can look into—and close the door. Don't worry about what your spouse, or kids, or others, think at this point. Now, please look into your mirror at the face of the awesome human being looking back at you, and repeat these words, "I am worthy of living a happy and successful life." That is good, but I want you to do it one more time. Please do it again, but this time, please say it like you mean it. Say it with conviction. **"I deserve to live a happy and successful life!"** How did that feel?

We have all come to this point in life with baggage from our childhood and disappointments from our lives. We all have limiting beliefs and other doubts that we face daily. Before you get much further into this book, I want you to know that I believe in you, and I am rooting for you. But, for this book to help you, you have to believe in yourself. You have to be rooting for yourself. You must know that you are worthy of living your ideal life. You deserve to have the life of your dreams.

Remember, you are a child of God. God makes no mistakes. Please trust me when I tell you that you are worth the time you are about to invest in reading this book and working through the personal reflection exercises at the end of each chapter that will help you create a design for your successful and happy life.

I wrote this book because it was the book I needed to read, but did not find, when I started out in life. My parents and stepparents were great, and did everything they could, but they were human just like we are. Mistakes were made and life goes on. I accidentally fell into a career in banking. It was not until my divorce, in 1987, that I started creating my life with intention. Yes, I have made mistakes along the way. Just know that you can overcome any obstacles you face—by first deciding you want to overcome them. Your future happiness begins in your thoughts. I don't claim to know all of the answers for your particular situation. What I do know for sure, however, is that you must care about yourself first in order to care for others on your journey and to live a happy and successful life. Now...let's talk about success for a minute.

CHAPTER TWO: THE MYTH OF SUCCESS

SUCCESS IS ELUSIVE

"Go to school. Get a job. Get ahead." These are the echoes of a society that thrives on success. We are encouraged to *do*, but rarely allowed to just *be*. It is interesting that our society places such a high value on success. Television and movies portray actors and sports figures as successful and happy. Yet, many of them are not happy. They drown their unhappiness in alcohol, drugs, sex, food, or other vices. Their cries for help go unnoticed. After all, they are successful, so they must be happy, right? Nothing could be further from the truth. It may surprise you to know that many people you know who appear to be successful and happy are really not very happy. Look around your office right now. How many people would jump at the chance to do something else if they knew it would pay them the same and provide some level of security?

Are you one of them?

When I announced my intention to leave my corporate job, most of my coworkers and employees stopped by my office to wish me well and confide in me that they were jealous that I was leaving. They told me they wished they had the guts to do the same. Perhaps fear stopped them, or perhaps their life's circumstances prevented a move at that moment. Whatever the reason, I found it very sad to know that the people I had worked with were, for the most part, unhappy—and even more sad, to know that they were afraid of taking action to improve their own situations and lives.

Society characterizes success by the attainment of some type of external goal. It may include getting or achieving wealth, respect, position, honors, or fame. *Merriam-Webster's Dictionary* defines success as, "the fact of getting or achieving wealth, respect, or fame." The ingredient missing from success is also missing from its definition. There is no mention of how success will make us feel. Although we all strive for some measure of success, there is nothing in this definition that tells us how success will feel once we have attained it. How will our lives change as a result? These are the things we don't know, and won't know until we have attained the goals we strive for.

Success is elusive. Most of the time, life doesn't turn out the way we think it should. And sometimes it turns out exactly the way we dreamed, but it was not what we thought it would be. After graduating from college, I was hired as a systems analyst for a major oil company in Houston, Texas. I climbed the corporate ladder through a series of strategic job changes and successful projects. I was making more money than I had ever made in my life. I had the corner office, the title, and the company car. I was the epitome of success, or so it seemed. Although I had achieved the level of success that I had strived for in my career, I was not happy. I was miserable, and I felt guilty about being so unhappy. I had it all, right? I should have been happy—but I wasn't. Why hadn't achieving all of that success guaranteed my happiness?

The reason success is so elusive is that we fail to define for ourselves what will truly make us happy. We get caught up in society's definition of what success should look like. We don't take time to reflect and think about what success should look like or feel like for *us*. My definition of success and happiness will be very different from your definition. It is personal. That is why you are the only one who can do this work. You must gain clarity about what a happy and successful life looks like for you.

I had a client one time who told me that figuring out what she really wanted was too hard. She could easily tell me what she didn't want, but she couldn't articulate what she did want. Guess what? This is a common problem. It is like the whack-a-mole game: by focusing on what we don't want, we actually bring more of it into our lives. Then we are constantly battling through those very things we don't want, but that we continue to focus on.

I had another client who was a successful photographer. She had started her business several years before, and had built a successful business. She was making enough money from her business to support her family. She was well-known and sought after in the community because of the quality of her work. In spite of her success, she was constantly in fear of running out of money. Her thoughts were constantly on worrying about not having enough. Her fear held her back. It kept her from making important investments and expanding and growing her business. By focusing on not having enough money, she actually kept her business from growing, which would have brought her more money and eliminated the need to worry about not having enough. Her inability to envision what it would be like to have more money effectively kept her in a constant spiral and state of worry.

To change our circumstances, we must first change our thoughts. We must gain clarity about those things we do want. When we do, we can focus on the right things and will attract more of them. Figuring out what you really want, and what will really make you happy, is hard. It may be the hardest thing you ever do.

As you go through this book, take the time to reflect and write down the answers to the questions I will pose. You can download the companion work-book to capture your thoughts. This is your opportunity to think through your true desires before you act. The people who are the most successful write down what they want. Don't skip this step.

Napoleon Hill, the author of *Think and Grow Rich*, was commissioned by Andrew Carnegie to document the Andrew Carnegie personal achievement formula. Mr. Carnegie arranged for Hill to interview 500 of the richest men of their time. Hill asked the men one question, and then captured and compiled their responses. The question was, "What is the secret of your success?" Without fail, a common response emerged:

1.　　　I write down my goals.
2.　　　I look at them every day.

If this advice is good enough for the wealthiest men in the world, it is good enough for me—and it should be good enough for you. The act of casting your desires to paper makes them more concrete. They become real. They are no longer rolling around in your head. Writing them down will help you gain clarity, and cause you to focus your mental energy—which in turn, will direct your physical activity. The act of writing down what you really want is the first step in achieving it. It is powerful, and as evidenced by Napoleon Hill's study, it works!

There is no secret magic-formula that draws a direct path from success to happiness. You have to create the path yourself. It starts in your mind.

WHAT IS SUCCESS, REALLY?

Most of us assume that attaining the goals that make us *successful* will also make us happy. This may be true in cases where an individual is lucky enough to also have a well-rounded life and supportive family, but it is also true that the act of achieving success will not, in and of itself, make you happy.

The fact is that nothing outside of you can truly make you happy. Not a person, or money, or a promotion. You may have a fleeting moment of happiness as a result, but it is fleeting. Life happens. People disappoint. Your favorite boss will leave. The company you work for will lay you off, or perhaps even close its doors. The economy will take another nosedive. The external trappings of success are just that—they are external, and for the most part, are out of your control.

Placing your faith in an external object or another person to make you happy is ill-conceived, and will eventually lead to disappointment. This is actually true not only in your career, but also in your life.

I have a friend named Dennis; he is a talented musician and songwriter, who tells a story of achieving his first success as a musician and being booked to go on his first tour of ten cities in the United States. His career was taking off, and he was getting the recognition for his work—that he so desperately craved. Success was finally his. And then one evening, Dennis called home to speak to his wife and son. When his wife put his son on the phone, the young child asked his father, "Daddy, when are you coming home?" Dennis's heart melted. At that defining moment, Dennis realized that society's measure of success did not include the ingredients that were going to make him happy. Dennis wanted to spend those precious years with his family, not on the road in a tour bus with a bunch of musicians. It was a defining moment for my friend, Dennis. He promptly got on the next bus, and headed home. Dennis's definition of success did not include giving up time with the people he loved. We always have a choice.

There must be more to being called *successful* than just attaining external goals. Our desire should be to have a well-rounded and happy life. I have found that to be happy, our lives must consist of a sense of purpose and a desire to serve others. Life must consist of loving relationships with God and with our family and friends. These are the things that make a life worth living. These are the only things that will make you happy. And these are the things that truly define success.

Again quoting from Napoleon Hill's classic, *Think and Grow Rich*:

Money and material things are essential for freedom of body and mind, but there are some who will feel that the greatest of all riches can be evaluated only in terms of lasting friendships, harmonious family relationships, sympathy and understanding between business associates, and introspective harmony which brings one peace of mind measurable only in spiritual values!

HAPPINESS IS A STATE OF MIND

Riches cannot always be measured in money! — Napoleon Hill

Happiness is a state of well-being, pleasure, contentment, or joy. Happiness is a feeling. Happiness is internal. You have to find it within yourself. You have to decide what happiness means to you. Happiness is found in our relationships with other people. It is found in the moments we create. It is built upon a life of purposeful living. *Being happy* is important to our physical and mental well-being.

Happiness is something you create. It is a state of mind. It is what you tell yourself every day when you get out of bed. You get to choose every day whether to be happy or unhappy. I choose happiness. What will you choose?

MAKE A DIFFERENCE

We are all mortal. Sorry to break that news to you. When you reach the end of your life, what will you see when you look back? How will others view you?

This may sound morbid, but humor me for one moment. Grab a piece of paper, and draw a picture of a tombstone. On it, write your birth date and death date. Let's imagine you will live to be 100 years of age or more. Of course, none of us are even guaranteed tomorrow. Now, write your epitaph. What will your tombstone say?

Copyright: Tony Baggett / 123RF Stock Photo

Here are some famous epitaphs for you to consider:

- Andrew Carnegie: *"Here lies a man who knew how to enlist the service of better men than himself."*
- John Cummings: *"If a man can tell he's been successful in his life by having great friends, then I have been very successful."*
- Will Rogers: *"If you live life right death is a joke as far as fear is concerned."*
- Harold J. Story: *"Before you jump in here with me, make sure you bring good memories. For here they're all we have to trade, and where you are is where they're made."*
- John Wayne: *"Tomorrow is the most important thing in life. Comes into us at midnight very clean. It's perfect when it arrives and it puts itself in our hands. It hopes we've learned something from yesterday."*

Perhaps yours will say something like, "Loving father, husband, son, and brother."

Is your life in alignment?

Would your family and friends agree with you?

If they would, that is great. Congratulations! If you are not sure, then also congratulations, because you have a unique opportunity to do something about it right now. Most people go through a significant life event before deciding they need to change. They have a near-death experience or experience the loss of a loved one.

Here is another quick exercise.

Write down your age in years, and multiply by 52 to get your current age in weeks. Now, subtract that number from 4056 weeks, which is the number of weeks in the average life expectancy of 78 years.

My age _____ (in years) x 52 weeks = _____ weeks.

4056 weeks - _____ = _____ weeks.

This is the average number of weeks you have left!

How will you spend them?

As I have already mentioned, a series of defining moments led me to discover that I was living my life in the wrong order and caused me to evaluate the purpose and meaning of my life. You don't have to have a significant life event to take stock of where you are, and decide to make a change. You only need to hold up the mirror to take a look right now.

Most of us have our priorities backward. We are so focused on making a living that we miss out on opportunities for happiness. True happiness comes when we focus first on making a difference for others, followed closely by making a life by spending time with the important people in our lives.

We all have an innate need to make a difference. To feel needed. To truly matter. To live a meaningful life. At the end of our lives, we want to look back and be able to say that our lives mattered. Unfortunately, most of us are just too wrapped up with the day-to-day grind of making a living, that we don't take time to consider whether we are truly making a difference, or whether our actions may be hurting those closest to us.

I have seen too many people working at a job, or running a business, that did not truly make them happy—and in fact, made them very unhappy. I have known many people like Ken. Ken has a good job, and makes good money working for a large Fortune 100 company. He goes to work every morning at 6:00 a.m., and leaves after 9:00 p.m., getting home every night after his two beautiful daughters go to bed. On the weekends, he is just too tired to do anything else but watch television or sleep. Sometimes, Ken even goes to the office on the weekend. He rarely finds time for his family. Last year, he was chosen to go on a company trip to Europe with several of the managers from his department. He decided to bring his family along with him so they could all see Europe together. But instead of spending quality time in the evenings with his family, he went out to dinner with his work colleagues. In other words, he did not see his family any more on this trip than he did back at home. What Ken may not realize, is that he is throwing his life away working for a company that does not really care about him—while missing out on the lives of the people that really DO care about him. Ken's two little girls are growing up without him. Does anyone else but me see the problem here?

When I discovered that I was unhappy with the trappings of success, I realized that my unhappiness stemmed from the fact that I didn't feel like what

I was doing really mattered. My need to contribute something meaningful to the world was greater than my need to stay safe and secure in my corporate job. So, I took a risk and started a business. I am not saying that this is the only avenue available to you to pursue happiness or meaning. I am only saying that this was the avenue I chose.

You may find meaning in your current role as a leader, employee, father, mother, husband, wife, son, daughter, church member, or volunteer. You will find meaning when what you do aligns with your values and beliefs.

As a business coach, I was blessed to work with inspiring business owners and leaders who truly desired to make a difference. It was always my pleasure to help them in their journey. I got to feel I was making a small difference by helping them make a difference to their employees, customers, and in their communities.

Linda Ellis, in her poem entitled, "The Dash" reminds us that it is not truly our birth day, or even the day we die that makes a difference. It is the way we live our dash. So, I ask you. How are you living your dash? Are you focused on the right priorities in your life?

> *Always I hear this inner voice: Is it enough? Did I do good? And sometimes if I'm quiet:* **Does it mean anything?**   *John Ortberg, When the Game is Over It All Goes Back in the Box.*

We all subconsciously want to feel that we have somehow made a difference in the world. The good news for us is we get to make that choice.

DESIGNING A LIFE

You would never start out to build a house without consulting an architect to create a blueprint plan. Why is it, then, that most people start out without a definite plan for their life? The information in this book will provide a blueprint for you to use to honestly reflect on where you are today, and to chart a course for where you want to be. You deserve to live your ideal life. Let's get started on your blueprint.

CHAPTER THREE: STEALING YOUR DREAMS: BARRIERS TO ACHIEVING YOUR IDEAL LIFE

WHY SELF-AWARENESS?

The first step in your journey is to assess your starting point. Since the journey begins in your mind, it makes sense that we first need to examine your thoughts. Self-awareness is a critical skill, and one found in all successful people. The art of being self-aware provides the opportunity to evaluate what is working, and what is not working, to make corrections. The truth is, our thoughts and actions are the only things we can control. We cannot control other people, but we can control our reaction to them.

TRUST MODEL

The goal of self-discovery is to find out what others see about us that we cannot see. We all have strengths, but when overused, our strengths can become our weaknesses. For example, two of my strengths are empathy and harmony; therefore, I don't like conflict. Used to excess, it becomes a limiting factor. If I am not aware of this tendency to avoid conflict, I may let things go that should be addressed. If my strength is determination, used to excess, I may become too demanding and run over people.

We must understand our blind spots to effectively communicate, increase trust, share ourselves, and minimize surprises. I have worked with some very talented people who had little quirks in their personalities that made them unbearable to be around. You probably have too. Our goal, therefore, is *not* to be that person.

Within the Trust Model, adapted from Luft and Ingham's Johari Window (*Introduction to Behavioral Analysis Online Course Certification Guide*, 2011, 6), there are four areas of interest.

Figure 1: The Trust Model Adapted from Luft & Ingham's Johari Window

WHAT OTHERS SEE		
WHAT YOU SEE	**ARENA** Area of Open Communication	**BLIND SPOT** Area of Self-Discovery
	MASK Hidden Area	**POTENTIAL** Unknown Area

Source: The Institute for Motivational Living, Inc. "The Trust Model Adapted from the Johari Window." *Introduction to Behavioral Analysis Online Course Certification Guide*, 2011, 6.

1. We have an arena of open communication, the known self, in which you and I both know.
2. We have a mask, which is the hidden self in which I know, but it is hidden from you, so you do not know.
3. We have blind spots, or areas of self-discovery, which you know, but I do not know.
4. Finally, we have an area of potential, or the unknown self, which is completely unknown to both of us.

The focus in most of this book will be to help you explore these areas, especially your blind spots or areas of self-discovery. This section will look at those areas that may reach out and steal your dreams.

YOUR COMFORT ZONE

In spite of your desire to make a difference, and to create a new vision for your life, the unfortunate truth is that there will be challenges. The good news and the bad news is that most of the challenges are within your own mind. I will explain, but first, please do this exercise.

Stand up and cross your arms comfortably. It should feel comfortable and natural. You did not have to think about it. It was automatic. A habit.

Copyright: nyul / 123RF Stock Photo

Now, reverse the position of your arms. Put your bottom arm on top.

It should feel awkward and unnatural. You had to think about the change.

Leaving your comfort zone will feel strange. Breaking old habits is not easy, but lasting and positive change requires you to extend yourself outside of your comfort zone.

Your comfort zone is where you spend most of your life. Think about it. We have a comfortable pair of shoes. Our chair is comfortable. Our job or career—even if we are not happy—is still comfortable.

It is all we know.

Why do you think that 70% of people who win the lottery are broke again within five years?

It is because their comfort zone does not include having and managing large sums of money. Your mind and body's natural resistance to change is to try to get back to the center of your comfort zone.

A good example of this is from my own struggle with my weight. I have probably gained and lost hundreds of pounds. I have gone on diets, lost weight, been happy with the results, and then reverted back to the old habits (comfort zone) that led to the weight gain to start with. To make a definite change requires us to change those habits and get uncomfortable. I now know that I cannot eat a bowl of ice cream every night and remain the size I want to be. I love ice cream. But, real and lasting change is worth the sacrifice.

To find the happiness you are looking for, you will experience some discomfort while escaping the confines of your comfort zone. There are tools and people to help.

Man is the center of an unending circumference. — Ghandi

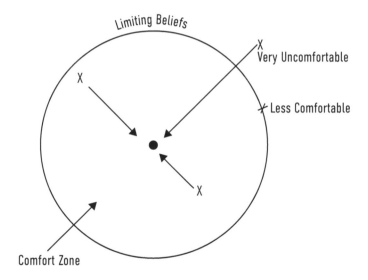

It is human nature to try to move back to the center of our comfort zone where it is comfortable. As we move farther away from the center, we become more uncomfortable. We are always striving to get back to the center. Real change occurs just outside of your comfort zone.

Trust me, once you are on the other side, it will be worth it. Embrace being uncomfortable. It is where breakthroughs occur.

YOUR MENTAL MODELS

Mental models include your values and belief systems about the way the world works. We have been forming mental models since we were babies.

Tied up in your mental model is your self-image and identity. Mental models are very handy in helping us navigate the world safely on autopilot much of the time.

But your current mental model is not reality. It is the picture in your mind of your *perception* of reality. Think of a mental model as the road map of the world you navigate. One way to put it into perspective is you can drive on the roads, but you cannot drive on the map.

Our mental models form the context for our world, and serve to help keep us safe. In performing this role of keeping us safe, however, they also present the barriers that prevent us from stepping outside of our comfort zone to find our happiness and often provide the basis for our unfounded fears.

To illustrate your mental models, think about a time you may have seen someone bungee jump, or jump out of a plane, or climb to the top of Mount Everest. Have you ever said to yourself, wow, I could NEVER do that! That is your mental model at work, thinking it is keeping you safe.

The reality is you CAN do that and more. You just have to envision what you want to do, and then go for it. Your thoughts precede your actions. You just have to form new mental models.

The barriers to your happiness exist first in your own mind as part of your mental models.

YOUR FUDS

FUDS are the fears, uncertainties, doubts, and suspicions that we all have. FUDS are negative and limiting beliefs. Most of our fears are never realized, yet they sometimes consume our thoughts. Common fears include the fear of death, fear of failure, and fear of public speaking. Did you know that the number one fear for most people is the fear of public speaking? And this is more fearful than the fear of death? Does that really make sense? The guy giving the eulogy is more fearful of giving the speech than of being in the box. Crazy, right?

Imagine, if you will for a minute, the very first time you were told that you would have to give an important presentation. It may have been at work or at school. You prepared and practiced the best you could, didn't you? Then what happened on the day of the presentation? Were you nervous? Did you imagine all sorts of things that might go wrong? Did you feel sick at your stomach? Did you think you might faint?

Then do you remember what happened? You gave your presentation, and you were brilliant. Remember? You overcame your fear and mastered that presentation. Perhaps you have given many presentations since then, or perhaps you still have a fear of public speaking. The point is, once you have mastered that first presentation, you are one step closer to overcoming the fear. You took one step outside of your comfort zone toward creating a new mental model. Overcoming a fear has that benefit. It helps us enlarge our comfort zones.

Perhaps you are uncertain about this whole idea of making a change. You have doubts about your ability to make a good living doing something else. Maybe you are just suspicious of my motives in telling you this. Rest assured, these are all normal reactions to the prospect of making a change. The battle is won or lost in our minds.

Yes, I understand that you have family obligations that may prevent you from taking a drastic step. I know you have bills to pay. I get that your spouse may think you are crazy. I have been there, and done all of that. What I will tell you is that the fear of taking a step can be crippling. But the regret of not taking that step will be worse. I will show you everything you need to know before you take that next step. Once you have clarity about your desire to create a new future—and know what your future holds because you have envisioned it—the steps become easier.

Take my hand. Let's take the next step forward into your future.

YOUR WILLINGNESS TO STRETCH YOUR BOUNDARIES

On your way home from work, do you drive in the slow lane or the fast lane? Every individual has a different tolerance for risk. Your personal risk-profile will determine your willingness to change jobs, start a business, or stay where you are. Your risk profile is inherently an individual trait. Be honest with yourself about your risk tolerance. Be sure you challenge any limiting beliefs that may be holding you back. The reality is that nothing is 100% fool-proof and safe. Jobs that seem safe can go away tomorrow when the company changes direction. Careers that were important ten years ago no longer exist, because the industry has changed.

As you decide your next move, factor your risk tolerance into the decision, but do not let it be the only factor you consider.

A short fun quiz to assess your investment risk-tolerance is included as a resource in the **Tools of Self Discovery** section of this book.

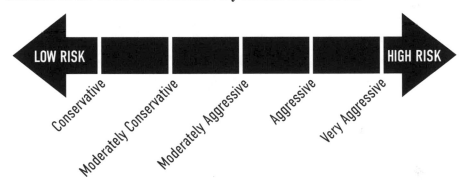

YOUR CLUTTER

Clutter can be defined as anything that takes up your time, and does not contribute directly to your goals. Sometimes we just get too busy being busy. We are so caught up in the illusion of busyness that we don't stop and ask if we are busy working on the *right* things. Most people struggle because they manage the time they have poorly. Often, finding more time is simply a matter of prioritizing the time we have.

I would like to point out here the difference between *effectiveness* and *efficiency*. Effectiveness is doing the right things. Efficiency is doing things right. You can get caught in the trap of doing the wrong things very efficiently. Don't do it. You really want to be effective with your time prioritization. Notice, I did not say *time management*. Time management is a myth. You cannot manage time. You can only prioritize the activities you fit into the time you have. Later in this book, I will share a priority management system that has worked for me.

If you are familiar with the Pareto principle, or the 80-20 rule, you know that 80% of our results usually come from 20% of our activities. We spend 80% of our time, working on trivial activities that are meaningless in the long run.

Successful people prioritize their time and energy on the activities that will bring them the most joy, success, happiness, and well-being. Unsuccessful people focus their time and energy on the activities that fill up their days, but do not take them toward their goals.

To be more effective, you must identify the clutter in your life so that you can prioritize, delete, downsize, or delegate it.

Some examples of clutter that have been identified by my past clients include email, television, excessive time on Facebook and other social media, excessive time on video games, looking for lost things, commuting to work, talking to telemarketers, hitting the snooze button on the alarm, doing other people's jobs, surfing the internet, reading junk mail, reading and re-reading mail or email, etc. I am sure you will think of something new.

YOUR BORDER BULLIES

Border bullies are those people and internal voices on the sidelines who will unintentionally derail your dreams and plans. They really don't mean any harm, and they honestly think they are helping. When you make a decision to change something in your life, the border bullies are there to say, "Are you crazy? You cannot do that." You have to learn to put the border bullies in their place. Acknowledge them for trying to help, and then put them away. For example, when I decided to join IDLife as a distributor, I did it because I loved the product and the financial opportunity it provided. I could see its value for changing people's health and financial well-being. The border bullies were in the background saying things like, "Aren't you embarrassed for joining a network marketing company?" At first, I listened to them. I kept my discovery about IDLife to myself. Then, I realized I was not helping anyone by keeping it a secret. My fear of being one of those annoying over-zealous salespeople had kept me from sharing the value of IDLife—both as a product and an opportunity—with those I loved. What a disservice to them! I vowed to keep the border bullies at bay, and help those I love by telling them what I was doing. It became their choice (and their problem) if they choose to ignore it. What I did not want was for them to come to me later to ask me why I never told them about it. So, keep your border bullies at bay by putting them in their place. Frankly, your spouse and your kids don't understand you any more than you understand them, so don't expect them to.

As you continue reading this book, the border bullies and all of your limiting beliefs and FUDS will appear from time to time. Be sure you have a strategy for dealing with them. Tell them to go away. You have important work to do here while you design your ideal life.

Now, get busy on the personal reflection section for this chapter.

PERSONAL REFLECTION

OVERCOMING THE BARRIERS THAT CAN STEAL YOUR DREAMS

In this section, we have covered the "gotchas" that can reach out and steal your dreams. If you have not already done so, please take a few moments of self-reflection to answer these questions.

In the section on FUDS, we discussed the *fears*, *uncertainties*, *doubts*, and *suspicions* that hold us back. Now is the time to confront your own fears. Answer these questions honestly. The first step to conquering a fear is to name it.

What are the limiting beliefs and fears holding me back?

- Fears
- Uncertainties
- Doubts
- Suspicions

- Have I ever tested these fears or limiting beliefs for accuracy?
- What is the absolutely worst thing that could happen if these fears materialize?
- What if I am wrong?

PERSONAL RISK TOLERANCE

Answer these questions to get a feel for your personal level of risk tolerance.
- When I hear the word risk, what comes to mind?
- Does risk seem dangerous or exciting?
- Am I willing to stretch my boundaries to learn new things, or try something new?
- Am I happier sticking to what I already know, and trying to find a new opportunity in the same industry?

CLUTTER

- What are the non-essential clutter and low-value distractions in my professional or personal life?
- For each of the items I listed, what commitments can I make to avoid, delegate, delay, downsize, or delete it?

BORDER BULLIES

- Who and what are the border bullies that I need to be aware of so I can keep them in their place?
- What is my strategy for dealing with border bullies?

CHAPTER FOUR:
DISCOVER YOUR STARTING POINT

EVERY JOURNEY BEGINS WITH A THOUGHT

If you woke up tomorrow and decided to go to Chicago, what is the first thing you would do? You would decide whether to take a plane or drive your car. You would decide which route to take. You would decide what day and time to leave. You would determine where to stay. And you would plan on when to come home, unless this was a permanent move to Chicago. The point in all of this is—your plans all began with an *idea*. The idea was "I am going to Chicago."

You must know where you are starting. If you are starting from Houston, you are taking a different route, than if you are starting in Seattle. Changing your life or career begins with a thought and requires some planning. You have to first decide to do it. You must decide—then do!

YOUR STARTING POINT

So far, I have described success and happiness, and why success, the way society defines it, is elusive and shallow. I have suggested to you that doing work that makes a difference will lead to a meaningful life, and I have also prepared you for the barriers you will find along the way—most of which you will find in your own mind.

Vision without execution is hallucination. — Thomas A. Edison

Now, if you are ready, I will take you on a journey of self-discovery. You will have more work to do as I take you through some tools and exercises to help you discover that one thing that you could do—if you choose to—that would give you joy, help you make a difference in the world, and help you create your ideal life.

Every journey begins with a starting point. You must know where you are coming from to plot a course toward your destination. The personal-reflection exercises that follow each chapter will take you through a quick self-evaluation. Grab your workbook, and write down your answers to the questions as you go through the book. Your current situation is how it is and what it is, because of decisions you have made. Now is the time. You must take 100% responsibility for your life.

> *You must take personal responsibility. You cannot change the circumstances, the seasons, or the wind, but you can change yourself. — Jim Rohn, America's foremost business philosopher*

Jack Canfield, author of *The Success Principles: How to Get From Where You are to Where You Want to be*, suggests that one of the most pervasive myths in American culture is that someone else is responsible for creating our happiness, providing career options and meaningful personal relationships. There really is only one person responsible for the quality of the life you live.

THAT PERSON IS YOU!

To make a change, you must change your mindset, your thinking, your behavior. You must change your ideas about yourself, your life, and your business or career.

Many of us have grown up and been conditioned to blame others for our circumstances or bad breaks. We blame our spouse, our parents, our teachers, our kids, our clients, our bosses, the media, the democrats, or even the government. We tend to want to blame anyone and everyone else. We never look where the real problem is—that is with ourselves.

Canfield tells a story of a young man who is out walking and comes upon another man on his knees, searching for something under a street lamp. The young man inquires of the man on his knees what he is searching for. The man replies that he was looking for his lost key. The passerby gets down on his knees and starts to help him look. They search high and low with no luck. Finally, the passerby asks, "Are you sure you lost it here?" The other man replies, "No, I lost it in my house, but the light is better out here under the street lamp."

It is time to stop looking outside of yourself to find the success and happiness you deserve. To achieve success and happiness, you must take 100% responsibility for your life.

This chapter will help determine your starting point, and set the stage for your future journey. Remember, working through the questions for each chapter will provide you the opportunity to reflect on areas of your life that may be painful to think about. That is okay. This is only the beginning. You must know your starting address to map the journey to your destination.

First, though, a word about the importance of reflection in helping you create the life you desire.

THE POWER OF REFLECTION

Reflection is the act of sitting in a quiet place and thinking deeply. The next few sections will provide a guide for you to reflect. As you read each section, and the questions that follow, close your eyes and think deeply before answering. Then, open your eyes and write YOUR answers. You must be honest and true to yourself to reap the benefits of this process. This is YOUR life, and these are YOUR answers. This is not about what you think you SHOULD do, or what someone else thinks, or even about what you think others will want to hear. This is your moment of truth. You are holding up the mirror to your life to perform an evaluation. Be honest with yourself. Are you ready to discover your future?

Honest self-reflection leads to self-awareness and growth.

FINDING THAT ONE THING

As Donald Clifton, author and creator of the Clifton Strengths Finder, was partial to saying: "Everyone does at least one thing better than 10,000 other people. That's the good news. The bad news? Most people have no idea what that one thing is."

YOUR WIRING

Every individual is made up of a unique blend of strengths, talents, abilities, interests, values, beliefs, motivations, personality, preferences, and emotions. Researchers call these our *individual differences*. I will refer to these differences as *your wiring*.

Understanding your wiring will help you understand the types of jobs and activities that you feel naturally drawn to, and that you might do for free, but would love to get paid for.

Our wiring presents a challenge, because its existence guarantees that what works for me won't work for you, and what works for you will not work for me. Our wiring is also the reason why most self-help books don't work. The author finds some magic formula that works for them to solve some problem, so they write a book. The reader buys the book, and tries the formula, but fails. He or she then says, I should have known it was just another self-help book that would not work.

The thing is, the book is not flawed. The approach is not flawed. It probably does work for some number of people who are wired similarly to the author who wrote it.

So my purpose in this section is to provide a proven method for you to discover your wiring, and hopefully identify what will work for you. I will lead you through some exercises and reflective questions. I will refer you to some outside resources that can help.

This is not a passive section. Reading this information and doing nothing else will not solve your problems. You must do the work. Get your book and pencil, download the workbook from the companion website (if you have not already done so), sit down, roll up your sleeves, and let's get to work on your future. In the next few sections, we will work on some exercises together to discover your "One Thing."

YOUR VALUES

What I know is, is that if you do work that you love, and work that fulfills you, the rest will come. And, I truly believe, that the reason I've been able to be so financially successful is because my focus has never, ever for one minute been money. — Oprah Winfrey

Your values are your core beliefs and deep needs. Values represent those things that truly matter most to you. I consider an understanding of your personal values foundational to creating the ideal life. Most people understand that they have values, but most people have not taken the time to sit down and think about which values are the most important to them. Everyone has a handful of values they will not compromise. Working in a job or business that we feel has violated our values makes us uncomfortable. It may even threaten our well-being.

For example, I place a high value on loyalty. When my employer began a systematic process of laying people off—a few every month—I was uncomfortable and disenfranchised. I place a high value on being loyal to my team and to my employer. When my employer did not reciprocate that loyalty to the people who worked for them, I found the situation intolerable. Some of the people had given them 30 years of loyal and valuable service. My values, and the values of my employer, were out of alignment. I found the situation intolerable, so I started looking for opportunities to leave.

When you work in a career or create a business in accordance with your values, you will be naturally happy as you work at it. And you will feel tremendous satisfaction with your work, so you will naturally be more successful and happy.

WHAT ARE VALUES?

Values are deep emotional states or feelings. For example, money is not a value. A value may be the feeling you get from money. That may be security, or freedom, or peace of mind. Money may be the means to achieve your value. For example, one client I worked with places a high value on security. Making money is the means to achieve that value. To get down to the core emotional state you desire, ask yourself, "What deep emotional belief does this satisfy?" The answer is likely to be a core value.

Examples of values include:

ABUNDANCE	DECISIVENESS	HARMONY	ORDER	SELF-DEVELOPMENT
ACHIEVEMENT	DRIVE	HEALTH	PEACE OF MIND	SERVICE
ACCOMPLISHMENT	ELEGANCE	HONOR	PERFECTION	SPIRITUALITY
ACCOUNTABILITY	EMPATHY	HUMOR	PLEASURE	TEAMWORK
ADVENTURE	EXCELLENCE	INDEPENDENCE	PRESTIGE	TRUST
AFFECTION	FAMILY	INFLUENCE	POWER	VALOR
APPROVAL	FINANCIAL SECURITY	INTEGRITY	PUNCTUALITY	VISION
ASSERTIVENESS	FLEXIBILITY	JUSTICE	RELATIONSHIPS	WEALTH
CHALLENGE	FREEDOM	LEARNING	RECOGNITION	WISDOM
COMPETITION	FUN	LOVE	SECURITY	
COURTESY	HAPPINESS	LOYALTY	SELF-ACCEPTANCE	

Your ideal life should align with your values. If your core value is free-dom, does your job or career provide you with the flexibility you desire? You may find that your values shift with age. For example, early in my career, I placed a higher value on achievement than I do today. Today, I place a higher value on freedom. What are your core values?

YOUR GIFTS AND TALENTS

In her book, *Do What You Love, The Money Will Follow* (New York: Dell Publishing, 1987, 7), Marsha Sinetar described work that she disliked as work that did not fit her personality, disposition, and aptitudes. She said, "*I know that work needs to fit my personality just as shoes need to fit my feet.*" Does your work fit you?

One of the elements of a successful career is being able to use your strengths and talents to perform meaningful work. Each of us is made up of a unique recipe of skills and talents. Often, it is difficult for us to see what our strengths and talents are. Sometimes, it is easier to view our strengths and tal-ents through the eyes of others who interact with us.

These are not easy questions to answer for ourselves. I have many clients who really struggle with knowing their own talents. The thing is—we need to know what we are good at (and what we are not good at) so we can focus our career or business choices in an area in which we have a shot at success.

A powerful tool for understanding your strengths is the Clifton Strengths Finder. Information on where to find this tool is located in the resources sec-tion of this book.

Self-awareness is a key attribute of successful people. I left a career where I was a very successful project manager and later the director of an application development group. I believed that my success in this career would translate into success in my newly chosen career of business coaching. While I did love coaching and teaching, I really did not like sales. And because I disliked sales, I was not very good at sales. I would sit in front of the phone and agonize over having to make a phone call to set up an appointment. I could envision all sorts of rejection and unpleasant consequences. My business suffered. My personal finances suffered. Finally, another coach and good friend of mine asked me, "Why are you doing this to yourself? If you are not happy doing this, and it is causing you so much pain, why are you doing it?" Had I taken a real honest look at what my own strengths were, instead of believing that my past success would just "show up" in my new career, I might have chosen differently. Or, I might have chosen to bring on a partner who was good at the things I was not good at. The point is, I thought I knew myself, but I didn't really know myself well until I tried something new and failed. Failure is part of the learning process. Understanding your talents is key to designing your ideal life.

YOUR HABITS

The dictionary defines a habit as an acquired behavior pattern, regularly followed, until it has become almost involuntary. Our habits determine our results. Success comes from a series of good habits repeated over and over again. That is the good news. The bad news is that failure also comes from a series of bad habits repeated over and over again. The difference between success and failure may be found in our habits. People who are successful adopt effective habits, and minimize bad habits.

Evaluate yourself honestly when it comes to your habits. For example, if I get stuck writing, I find myself in front of the refrigerator looking for comfort food. Obviously, this bad habit is a form of procrastination and is not helping my weight. Confronting your bad habits is the first step in eliminating them. Just as important, however, is understanding your good habits so you can do more of them. I am a planner. I write lists and check things off. I plan the week ahead every Sunday afternoon. If I take this time, my week goes much smoother and I accomplish more than if I neglect this good habit.

Stephen R. Covey, author of the book, *7 Habits of Highly Effective People*, outlines habits of successful people. How many of Covey's habits have you adopted?

Habit 1: Be Proactive

Habit 2: Begin with the End in Mind

Habit 3: Put First Things First

Habit 4: Think Win-Win

Habit 5: Seek First to Understand, Then to be Understood

Habit 6: Synergize

Habit 7: Sharpen the Saw

What are some of your habits?

- Overeating
- Procrastination
- Exercise
- Making follow-up calls
- Finishing what you start
- Prayer
- Planning and goal setting
- Smoking
- Drinking in excess
- Expressing gratitude
- Calling your mom every Sunday

Honestly evaluate your habits, and make sure they are moving you toward your ideal life.

PERSONALITY

Every individual is unique in their intellect, personality, and emotions. Perhaps you have known people that you believed were "super smart" or people you felt were "volatile." Your individual differences should be considered when choosing your future path.

Gaining an understanding of your own personality and preferences will help you know how you are wired. You are perfectly suited for certain jobs, and not so suited for others. Knowing this information can help you plan your life, and choose a career in the areas in which you are more likely to succeed.

Gaining an understanding of other's personality and preferences will help you become a more successful communicator.

Assessments are available to help. Perhaps you have taken an assessment in the past. The DISC profile, or Myers Briggs assessments, are popular in many workplaces. I highly recommend you seek out one of the "official" assessment instruments. Many of these are available online, and are described in the section entitled **Tools of Self Discovery** in the resources section of this book.

BEHAVIOR PREFERENCES

Behavioral style is how others observe our behaviors. Our primary style tells us how we are motivated, points to the types of environments we may prefer, suggests how we communicate, provides insight into our fears, and gives insight into how we like others to communicate with us. Gaining an understanding of your behavior preferences will help you:

- Become a better communicator.
- Be able to effectively resolve or prevent conflicts.
- Gain credibility and be able to influence others positively.

As you go through your life and career, you will observe each of four behavioral styles.

Recognition of four different types of behavior dates back before the time of Christ to at least 400 B.C. when Hippocrates suggested four temperaments he named Sanguine, Melancholic, Choleric, and Phlegmatic. In the 1920's, Carl Jung defined four types of personality. In 1928, William Marston, a psychology professor at Columbia University, published a book called The Emotions of Normal People (New York: Harcourt Brace, 1928), in which he identified four behavior styles, classified as Dominance, Inducing, Steadiness, and Compliance, resulting in the acronym DISC. Walter Clark developed the first assessment based on Marston's theory in the 1950's. Since the 1950's, many individuals and companies have contributed to the current DISC model. The

DISC factors are aligned with the temperaments identified by Hippocrates and are generally described as follows:

The D (Dominance) factor measures how people respond to problems and challenges. The Dominance factor is comparable to Hippocrates' Choleric temperament.

The I (Influence) factor measures how people influence others to their point of view. The Influence factor is comparable to Hippocrates' Sanguine temperament.

The S (Steadiness) factor measures how people like consistency and respond to the pace of their environment. The Steadiness factor is comparable to Hippocrates' Phlegmatic temperament.

The C (Compliance) factor measures how people prefer to respond to rules and procedures set by others. The Compliance factor is comparable to Hippocrates' Melancholy temperament.

You can think of your DISC style as a representation of your preferences. There are no good or bad preferences, but understanding the differences will lead to improved communication and understanding. An example of a preference is whether you are right-handed or left-handed. You may be right-handed, but if you needed to learn to use your left hand you could do it. You are not restricted to using one area of preference. You can learn to adapt and adjust as needed. DISC does not measure intelligence levels, values, skills, experience, education levels, or training. What DISC does measure is an individual's observable preferred manner of doing things.

According to Marston, "All people exhibit all four behavioral factors in varying degrees of intensity" William Marston cited in Bonnstetter, Bill J., and Judy I. Suiter. The Universal Language, DISC: A Reference Manual (Phoenix: Target Training International, 2004, 38).

BEHAVIOR STYLES

Read through the adjectives used to describe each style in Table 1 and the descriptions that follow to see if you can determine your behavioral preference.

Table 1: DISC Adjectives

D	I	S	C
FORCEFUL	EXPRESSIVE	RESTRAINED	COMPLIANT
STRONG-MINDED	EMOTIONAL	SATISFIED	CAREFUL
PIONEERING	INFLUENTIAL	EASY MARK	CORRECT
DOMINEERING	ATTRACTIVE	WILLING	PRECISE
DETERMINED	STIMULATING	EVEN-TEMPERED	FUSSY
DEMANDING	CAPTIVATING	PATIENT	TIMID
SELF-RELIANT	COMPANIONABLE	KIND	OPEN-MINDED
PERSISTENT	PLAYFUL	SELF-CONTROLLED	AGREEABLE
HIGH-SPIRITED	TALKATIVE	GOOD-NATURED	SOFT-SPOKEN
IMPATIENT	CONVINCING	CONTENTED	RESIGNED
AGGRESSIVE	GOOD MIXER	GENTLE	RESPECTFUL
NERVY	POISED	ACCOMMODATING	CONVENTIONAL
ARGUMENTATIVE	CONFIDENT	RELAXED	COOPERATIVE
RESTLESS	INSPIRING	CONSIDERATE	WELL-DISCIPLINED
COURAGEOUS	OPTIMISTIC	SYMPATHETIC	DIPLOMATIC
POSITIVE	EAGER	LENIENT	EXACTING
ADVENTUROUS	ENTHUSIASTIC	LOYAL	ADAPTABLE
WILL POWER	ENTERTAINING	GOOD LISTENER	HUMBLE
COMPETITIVE	LIFE-OF-THE-PARTY	OBEDIENT	TOLERANT
VIGOROUS	PERSUASIVE	NEIGHBORLY	CAUTIOUS
OUTSPOKEN	ELOQUENT	RESERVED	STRICT
DOGGED	ANIMATED	OBLIGING	DEVOUT
ASSERTIVE	GREGARIOUS	NONCHALANT	DOCILE
BOLD	OUTGOING	MODERATE	PERFECTIONIST

DOMINANCE (CHOLERIC)

Individuals high in the Dominance factor actively confront problems and challenges while individuals low in the Dominance factor prefer to do more research before making a decision. People with a high Dominance factor may be described by others as demanding, driving, aggressive, strong-willed, and decisive.

INFLUENCE (SANGUINE)

Individuals high in the Influence factor are talkative and often emotional. They are described by others as sociable, spontaneous, funny, persuasive, political, and warm, and are often known as the "the life of the party."

STEADINESS (PHLEGMATIC)

Individuals high in the Steadiness factor prefer security, work at a steady pace, dislike change, and display little outward emotion. They are described by others as reserved, relaxed, patient, and consistent.

COMPLIANCE (MELANCHOLY)

Individuals high in the Compliance factor are conscientious, analytical, and adhere to structure and rules. They are described by others as cautious, accurate, tactful, careful, and detail-oriented.

If you are still unsure of your behavioral preference, DISC assessment instruments are referenced in Tools of Self Discovery in the resources section of this book, or can be found on the companion website. I highly recommend finding and taking one or more of the official assessments. Enter your thoughts in your personal-reflection workbook.

YOUR MOTIVATION

What motivates you? Everyone is motivated by something, but because of individual differences and culture, not everyone is motivated the same way. One of the most frustrating things on the planet is trying to figure out why someone is *not* motivated. The problem is that they are just motivated differently than we are. You are motivated differently than I am. That is the primary reason why I cannot give you the answers for your life. You have to discover the answers for yourself. It is also the reason why in a team of sales people, one person will be a superstar, and another will be content to rock along making the minimums. Perhaps the superstar is motivated by the money and competition. Perhaps the rocker is not motivated by money and is demotivated by the competition. If your sales incentive program does not recognize both motivating factors and provide incentives to satisfy both motivations, the rocker will just keep rocking along, and possibly fizzle out along the way.

It is also frustrating as a leader or a parent when the people we lead, or our children, do not seem to be motivated. The problem is that they are just not motivated the same way we are. If we can find that trigger for them, they will amaze us. If you understand how you are motivated, you can place yourself in situations in which you can succeed. Go ahead and complete the questions in the motivation section inside the personal-reflection section at the end of this chapter to gain insight into how you are motivated.

YOUR PERSONAL FINANCES

Whether you are a business owner or employee, you need to take stock once in a while about how you are doing financially. Are you financially fit? Do you have enough money, or would you like to have more? Are you struggling with debt? How is your credit rating? Could it be better? Go ahead and complete the information regarding your current financial situation, and your desired financial situation, in the personal-reflection section. This provides a snapshot of where you are right now.

YOUR PROFESSION

Many of us landed in a career by accident. Perhaps, you are still working at the job you took right out of school because it feels safe and it is all you know. In some cases, you may absolutely love what you're doing, and have no desire to do anything else. In other cases, you may have never felt quite at home in the career you hold, and you cannot wait to do something else. Perhaps you are counting the days until retirement so you can do something you have always wanted to do, but couldn't. Whatever the reason or situation, be honest with yourself. Answer the questions in the personal reflection section of this chapter.

YOUR CURRENT JOB

Sometimes we are in the right career, but not the right company or the right role within the industry. Take stock of what you love or hate about your current job, boss, or company while answering the questions in the personal reflection section of this chapter.

YOUR UNRESOLVED ISSUES

We all have unresolved issues or "messes." These may be things you have left undone, people you have hurt, relationships that need to be mended, or any other emotional or psychological thing that is weighing on your mind. My mess was getting my weight under control. At one point in my life, I weighed 205 pounds. I am now happily living a healthier lifestyle, and am on my way to a healthier weight.

I had one client who had not spoken to her brother in ten years. She could not even remember why they had argued. After our work together, she reached out, and as a result of her initiative, their relationship was mended. She was able to travel cross-country to spend the holidays with him and his family. Shortly thereafter, her brother died of a heart attack. Can you just imagine how this poor woman would have felt if her brother had died with this unresolved issue in their relationship? For the rest of her life, she would have regretted not having reached out to him.

Another client had an unpaid debt from a friend, which had weighed on my client's mind, and caused her to become estranged from a person she had once cared about. She just could not shake the feeling that her friend had compromised their friendship by not paying the debt. My client resolved to call the friend and tell her that the debt was forgiven and to consider it a gift. This freed my client from worrying about the unpaid debt, and opened the door for an important friendship to resume.

Maybe there is an employee issue that you have avoided taking care of because you did not want to have a hard conversation with the person. Perhaps you have broken a promise to someone, and you just need to apologize.

How about you? Do you have an unresolved mess you need to fix? If you do, 'fess up. Write your mess in the personal reflection section of your workbook.

YOUR LIFE BALANCE

As you focus on creating an ideal life of success and happiness, it is important to maintain your life balance. You can commit to changing your unbalanced life right now. In the personal-reflection section, you will find an exercise called the *Wheel of Life*. If you find your life out of balance, resolve to make the needed changes to get your life back in balance.

PERSONAL REFLECTION

MY VALUES

- What do I know, for sure, are my values?
- What values have I neglected?

MY GIFTS AND TALENTS

Reflect on the following questions and answer to the best of your ability. You may also share these questions with someone who knows you well, and ask them to honestly assess you. You may be surprised when you learn what they see about you that you cannot see for yourself. Answers to these questions will help you discover work in which you can be genuinely *you*.

- What are my top strengths and talents?
- What are my unique qualities?
- Why do current employees, staff, clients, and customers continue to interact with me?
- Why do people enjoy working with me?
- What attributes do I exhibit that make me likable?
- What would associates say are my natural gifts or talents?
- Why do new clients/customers choose to do business with me?
- What do I do for fun?
- What are my hobbies?
- What sports do I participate in?
- What gives me the greatest results with the least amount of time and effort?
- What activities do I do effortlessly that energize me and produce extraordinary results?
- What would I do for free, but would love it if someone would pay me to do it?

MY HABITS

- What are my top seven effective habits?
- What are the benefits of these habits?
  Make a commitment to yourself to maximize these good habits. They are helping you achieve your goals.
- What are my top seven ineffective habits?

- What are the consequences of these habits?

Make a commitment to yourself to minimize or eliminate these bad habits. They are taking you away from achieving your goals.

MY BEHAVIOR PREFERENCE

Review the discussion about behavior styles in the previous section, and then answer the following questions.

- What is your primary behavior style?
- What are the strengths of your behavioral style?
- What possible limitation of your behavioral style should you be aware of?
- Given what you know about your primary style, what types of careers might be a good fit?
- Given what you know about your primary style, what types of careers should you probably avoid?
- What insights have you learned about yourself from this exercise?

MY MOTIVATION

Your behavioral preferences provide clues to your motivation. Answer these questions about your motivation.

I am happiest when I:

1. Achieve measurable results
2. Gain recognition for my achievements
3. Am liked by others
4. Produce work that is accurate

My greatest fear is:

1. Loss of control
2. Loss of respect
3. Confrontation
4. Embarrassment

When working with other people, I like to be more:

1. Competitive

2. Cooperative

I prefer to:

1. Maintain the status quo

2. Make changes

I feel more valued at work when:

1. My boss expresses sincere appreciation

2. I receive a financial bonus

MY FINANCES

	MY CURRENT PERFORMANCE LEVEL:	MY DESIRED FUTURE PERFORMANCE LEVEL:
SALES/REVENUE		
ANNUAL INCOME		
PERSONAL DEBT		
BUSINESS DEBT		
SAVINGS		
INVESTMENTS		
BUSINESS VALUE		
WORK HOURS PER WEEK		
CREDIT SCORE		

- Do you feel fairly compensated for the work you do and for the hours you are working? If not, why not?
- Do you manage your household finances with a budget? If not, why not?
- Are there spending habits that you need to change?

MY PROFESSION

- Why did I go into my current career, profession, or business?
- What do I like about my profession?
- What do I dislike about my profession?
- If money and time were no object, would I still choose this career? If not, why not?
- What is the one thing I would change about my profession if I could?

MY CURRENT JOB

- What is working great in my company, department, and area of responsibility?
- What is broken in my company, department, and area of responsibility?
- What do I like about my role/area of responsibility?
- What do I dislike about my role/area of responsibility?
- What is the one thing I would change about my job if I could?

MY MESSES

What are some unresolved issues or "messes" in my personal or professional life?

MY LIFE BALANCE

A visual way to assess your life balance is a tool created by Zig Ziglar, called the *Wheel of Life*. Each of the spokes on the wheel represents an area of your life. The spokes represent a ten-point scale. Toward the hub approaches zero, while toward the outside approaches ten. Rate yourself on each area of your life by placing an *x* on each *spoke* of your life. Once you have done that, connect the x's by drawing a connecting line. You should end up with a wheel (or perhaps a flat tire).

Figure 2: Zig Ziglar's Wheel of Life

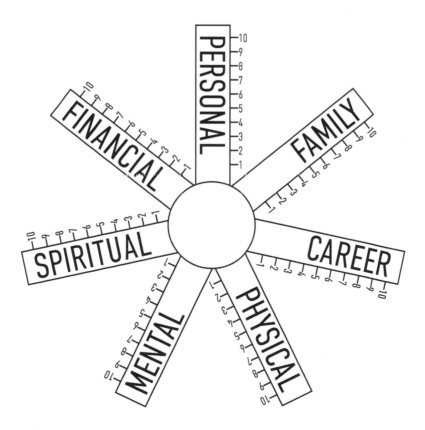

Zig Ziglar and Tom Ziglar. *Born to Win: Find Your Success Code.* Ziglar Inc., 2014. Ziglar.com

Now, looking at your honest assessment of your life, is your life in balance?

- What area(s) of my life is (are) out of balance?
- Where am I falling short?
- Whom have I helped?
- Whom have I hurt?

You have just plotted a starting point. Your past does not define you. In the next chapter, you will create the blueprint for your ideal life.

CHAPTER FIVE: DREAM YOUR FUTURE

THE FEELING IS "THE THING"

Maybe we have the questions all wrong. When I was growing up, my parents would ask me, "What do you want to be when you grow up?" Growing up I wanted to be a veterinarian or a teacher. Then I fell into my career with a job at a bank and became a banker. After my divorce I went back to school, I became a systems analyst, a programmer, a project manager, a manager, an executive ...well you get the idea. The questions I asked myself were things like, "What College should I attend?" "What major should I choose?" "What career should I pick?" "What job will I take?" I never once asked the most important question.

Danielle LaPorte asks the most important question in her book, *The Fire Starter Sessions*. Her question really caused me to stop and think. Danielle's question caused me to realize I had been asking the wrong questions. The question Danielle asked was, *"How do you want to feel in your life?"* I never asked how my career choices would make me feel. I focused on the *what*, not the *feeling*.

Instead of asking what you should do, ask how you want to feel. Then, back into what you need to do, in order to feel that way. For example, I am motivated by a desire to feel appreciated. Knowing that, I am able to place myself into situations to gain that feeling. I am also aware of my tendency to want to be liked instead of being valued. There is a difference. People who value you have no problem paying you for the value you deliver. People who like you expect you to share for free. Or perhaps, the real problem was my own mindset, because I wanted to be a friend, I sometimes would not charge my clients for my full value. Whatever the case, because I want to be liked, I almost bankrupted myself giving my valuable services away. Don't let that happen to you. The feeling is important, yes, but only when you are aware of how it affects your decisions.

Spend some time reflecting and thinking about how you want to feel. Look back at your behavior preferences for a clue.

D - Dominant/Direct — Are you results-driven and motivated by feeling in charge?

I - Influence – Are you recognition-driven and motivated by feeling admired and having fun?

S - Steady – Are you appreciation-driven and motivated by feeling liked and having friendships?

C - Conscientious – Are you fact-driven and motivated by feeling right?

As we move through the next section to create the blueprint for your ideal life, be sure you remember how you want to feel. At the end of the day, the feeling is "the thing" you are really looking for. Happiness is a feeling.

YOUR FUTURE BEGINS IN YOUR THOUGHTS

In his classic book, *Think and Grow Rich*, Napoleon Hill reminds us that our future is created in our thoughts. As we go through the next sections, you will be creating the blueprint for your ideal life. Some people will call this your vision. You will be thinking deeply about your desires in eight areas of your life. I call these areas the **8 Pillars of Your Ideal Life**. Having an ideal life involves balance between these areas. Sometimes, we get out of balance. Perhaps when you reflected in the previous section, you found that your life was out of balance. You get the chance to correct that here.

What I have discovered is many people struggle with visioning. They just cannot envision what a better life will look like. They can tell me what they don't want, but they cannot verbalize what they do want. The purpose of the 8 Pillars, and the process to create a blueprint for your ideal life, is to provide you with a method to create more than a vision, but a complete blueprint for your life. From your blueprint, you can begin to create your action plan.

CLARITY BEGINS WITH YOUR VISION OF THE IDEAL LIFE

It is not in the stars to hold our destiny but in ourselves. — William Shakespeare

Since you alone are responsible for bridging the path from success to happiness, and the path begins in your mind—it is important to have a clearly defined image in your mind of what you really want to achieve.

I am not telling you that it is bad to have success that includes wealth, or fame, or recognition. What I am telling you is that those things alone, are not enough. As we have explored, your life must also have meaning. Your happiness will stem from your ability to make a difference in the lives of others. Everyone desires to have significance, to achieve fulfillment, and to belong to something greater than themselves. Perhaps you have just not given it much thought, until now.

Despite what society believes, or even what I believe, you will have your own definition of success and happiness.

Grab your workbook and answer this question. Spend at least 30 minutes thinking about this and writing whatever comes to mind. Don't try to edit your thoughts. Just let them flow.

If you had all the time, and all the money, and all the resources, and all the contacts, and all the talent, and everything you need, and you wanted to design your life and career or business perfectly, what would it look like five years from now?

Now, close your eyes and really think hard about this; paint a vivid picture in your mind. Imagine what it would be like to achieve the level of success you are working for. How will it feel when you finally achieve it? How will you celebrate? Who will be there with you?

Come back to this page later as thoughts come to you, so you can jot them down. Create a vivid picture of the life you want to have.

To have the life you truly desire, you must start with the end in mind. Your thoughts precede your actions. You must be able to envision it first before you can create it.

Your must gain clarity around the people and things that really matter to you. If you struggled with painting a picture in your mind, you are not alone.

The next few sections will lead you through the process of exploring the 8 Pillars of Your Ideal Life. As you go through these sections, really think about these areas of your life, to ensure you arrive at the end with valuable insight into your future. When you write down your answers, remember to ask yourself how they make you feel. Then, write down your feelings, too.

If you gain clarity and focus, set goals for your life in the manner I describe in this book, and take action, it can propel you into the future you want. Now...let's look at the 8 Pillars.

8 PILLARS OF YOUR IDEAL LIFE

The 8 Pillars of your ideal life represent a fundamental precept upon which you can design the life of your dreams. Merriam-Webster defines a pillar as:

1 a : a firm upright support for a superstructure
   b : a usually ornamental column or shaft; especially : one standing alone for a monument
2 a : a supporting, integral, or upstanding member or part <a pillar of society>
   b : a fundamental precept <the five pillars of Islam>
3 : a solid mass of coal, rock, or ore left standing to support a mine roof
4 : a body part that resembles a column

The Parthenon still stands in Greece because of the strong pillars. So, building your life on strong pillars is a metaphorical way to make sure you don't overlook any foundational areas as you create the blueprint for your ideal life.

The 8 Pillars of Your Ideal Life include:

1. Health
2. Money
3. Relationships
4. Service
5. Spirituality
6. Gratitude

7. Time

8. Career/Business

Your 8 Pillars combined, create the vision for your ideal life. You may wonder why I listed Career/Business last, when it is such an integral part of our lives. I want you to think deeply about every other area of your life first, then when you think about your career or business, you will envision one that will support the ideal life you desire. Now, get ready, and let's go.

HEALTH

Health is like money, we never have a true idea of its value until we lose it. — Josh Billings

The first pillar of your ideal life is your health. Your health, in fact, is the most basic of the pillars. Without your health, no amount of money will be worthwhile. Ask a lifelong smoker who is dying of cancer about the choices he made, and whether it was worth it. Maybe it was, maybe it wasn't. The point is that we all have those choices to make. Our daily choices affect our long-term and short-term health. Have I always made healthy choices? Honestly, no. You may recall I mentioned in an earlier section that I once weighed 205 pounds. I am only 5'5", so I was really big for my height. But, after a friend's comment about a picture of me on Facebook, I took a hard look at myself, and realized that I was kidding myself into thinking that I just was not that big. That friend probably does not know that their words changed my life. In fact, their words were quite hurtful at the time. You know what they say, though, the truth hurts. Yes, it does. But if true friends tell you the truth, you should listen to them. Now at least, when I make an unhealthy choice, I know the choice I have made is not in alignment with my 8 Pillars. It is still my choice. It is your choice, too.

Disclaimer before we move on: I am not a doctor or a health professional. But, I do know about the importance of health. Your life is not a reality show... it is real and you only get one shot. A healthy lifestyle consists of a series of essential healthy habits. Are your habits creating greater vitality and health, or are they draining your battery and putting you at risk for disease? The choices you make every day add up to a lifetime of health or disease. Dr. Wayne Scott Andersen, author of *Dr. A's Habits of Health: The Path to Permanent Weight Control & Optimal Health* (Annapolis, MD: Habits of Health Press, 2008), says that in the U. S. alone, excess weight, obesity, and inactivity are responsible for 300,000 deaths each year—including complications caused by poor nutrition habits and obesity, such as type 2 Diabetes, coronary heart disease, osteoarthritis, stroke, and certain cancers. Obviously, no one wants to choose to be one of these gruesome statistics, yet our unhealthy habits have caused this epidemic.

When creating your Pillar for Health, areas to consider include exercise, diet, nutritional supplements, sleep, a positive environment, your energy level, your mind, and support. You may want to consider improvements such as losing weight or removing habits such as smoking, alcohol, drug use, or other habits you know are not healthy. Again, the choices are all yours.

How do you want to look and feel in 3-5 years? Write down your vision for your health pillar in the area provided for personal reflection in your companion workbook. Your vision will become the basis for goals that you will create for your action plan in the next section.

MONEY

Money is not everything, but it ranks right up there with oxygen.
— Zig Ziglar

Are rich people smarter, luckier, or more ambitious than the rest of us? Or, could it be that they just know things that we could know? The equation for having enough money is simple, isn't it? Yet many of us struggle with it.

Here it is: cash in (+), minus (-) cash out, equals (=) money left over at the end of the month. Or, put another way, income (+) minus expenses (-) equals (=) free cash flow.

While money can't buy happiness, it sure helps us enjoy life a bit more. Envisioning your financial well-being is a critical first step toward having financial well-being. If you cannot see a life in the future with no worries about money, it will be virtually impossible to have that life. Remember the whack-a-mole game? If your focus is on never having enough money, or on having things instead of money, you are destined to a life of "just enough" or perhaps a life of "never enough." Money is not a value, but money does provide freedom, or security, or other values you may have listed earlier in the book. Money is both emotional and cognitive. You have to learn that both your *beliefs* about money and your *behaviors* are in your control. Your beliefs include your thoughts, feelings, opinions, and expectations. Your behaviors include your spending, saving, and investing habits.

I am not a financial expert, but I do know, through personal experience, getting out of debt is hard, but can be done. If you struggle with money, get a financial advisor or someone else to help you plot a course to get your financial life back on solid footing. One of the best things I ever did was hire a financial advisor. For years, I thought I was smart enough to handle money. Why should I hire someone to do something I could do myself? Guess what? I was doing a terrible job with my money. I made poor choices. I spent more than I made. I consistently lived above my means. Here is the other confession. My family never knew how bad things were. I hid it from them. I was in debt up to my eyeballs, but my family never knew my pain. You see, in my family, we did not talk about money. Telling my family about my failures with money would be an admission that I was not as smart as they thought I was. Please don't make the mistakes I made.

Changing your financial habits is challenging. If your habit has been to live beyond your means by charging on your credit cards, the first step will be deciding not to do that any more. The second step will be to have a plan to increase your income enough to pay off those credit cards and begin to live within your means. The key to having enough money is to live within your means while increasing your means. The good news is that increasing personal income is within the grasp of everyone who chooses to do it.

Jim Rohn tells us that, *"Profits are better than wages."* What does this mean? It means that having a small business, even a part-time business, can lead to a fortune for someone willing to work at it. Wages are the result of swapping hours for dollars. You are limited in the number of hours you can swap, which limits your income. This is fine, if you resign yourself to living within those means. Just know that this decision will always limit your income, and keep you tied to working on someone else's dream. Your path to financial freedom is to increase your means by owning a small business, even if it is only part-time to start out.

Robert Kiyosaki provides advice I wish I had paid attention to sooner in my life. In his Cash Flow Quadrant, Kiyosaki shows the difference between linear income and residual income. On the left side of the quadrant, are employees and self-employed business owners. Both are limited by the amount of time they can spend swapping hours for dollars. On the right side of the quadrant are business owners and investors. Business owners leverage other people to make income. You are probably working for a business owner at your job. Investors put their money to work for them. Your goal should be to move into the business owner and investor categories as quickly as possible to have income that is not dependent on your physical presence.

Figure 3: Rich Dad's Cashflow Quadrant

EMPLOYEE	BUSINESS OWNER
You have a job	You own a system and people work for you
Trade time for money	Build an asset
Value steady income and benefits	Unlimited income potential
Income is limited by time	Income flows whether you work or not
SELF-EMPLOYED	**INVESTOR**
You own a job	Money works for you
Trade time for money	Unlimited income potential
Income is limited by time	Income flows whether you work or not

Kiyosaki, Robert T., and Sharon L. Lechter. *Rich Dad's Cashflow Quadrant: Rich Dad's Guide to Financial Freedom* (New York, NY: Warner Books, 1999).

While network marketing has endured a bad reputation over the years due to unscrupulous operators, the fact is that network marketing or direct sales, as it is also known, provides a low-cost way for anyone to move quickly into the business-owner category. There are hundreds, if not thousands, of network-marketing companies to choose from. Do your homework, and choose the one that you believe in and that fits your personality. Work the company's proven systems and don't give up. No business will work for you if you don't work the business. Network marketing is not a get-rich-quick scheme. Network marketing provides a vehicle for anyone who wants to work hard for 24-36 months to achieve a substantial income. Traditional business ownership is out of the reach of many people, and in a traditional business, if you stop working, your business stops working. Many well-known successful people, like Robert Kiyosaki and Donald Trump, have endorsed network marketing as an avenue to attain business ownership. My goal here is not to sell you on network marketing, but to show you that you have within your grasp an avenue to reach your financial dreams. You can attain financial fitness and build wealth with a part-time income, but first, you need to envision what that life will look like.

You must begin to understand, therefore, that the present state of your bank account, your sales, your health, your social life, your position at work, etc., is nothing more than the physical manifestation of your previous thinking. If you sincerely wish to change or improve your results in the physical world, you must change your thoughts, and you must change them immediately. — Bob Proctor, Author of the Power to Have It All

In an earlier section of this book, you captured a snapshot of your current personal finances. Now is the time to envision how you really want your financial life to look in three to five years. Write down the vision for your money pillar in the area provided for personal reflection in your companion workbook. Your vision will form the basis for goals that you will create for your action plan in the next section.

RELATIONSHIPS

Personal relationships are the fertile soil from which all advancement, all success, all achievement in real life grows. — Ben Stein

How are your relationships? Relationships are the pillar that makes life worth living. Healthy relationships with our family, friends, and the other people we come in contact with are important for our emotional well-being as well as our success. We must make time for the people we love today, because no one is guaranteed tomorrow. Are you spending enough time with the people you love? Would they agree with your answer to that question?

I attended a presentation last week where the presenter, Robin Roberts, passed out an exercise and challenged everyone with this question:

Imagine that you have just learned that you have only twenty-four hours to live. Within those twenty-four hours, you can do anything you want to do. You will have the skills you need. Money is no object. What would you do? Take the next two minutes and write down everything you would do in your last twenty-four hours.

What would your answer be? Go ahead and take a few minutes now and write your answer to this question.

I wrote down my own answer, and then I glanced at the paper of my friend, who was sitting next to me. She had written exactly one thing. Her answer said, "Spend time with family."

What did your answer say? You see, my friend wrote this because on a Friday morning two years ago, she lost her two youngest sons in a freak automobile accident. They left for school and work that morning, and that was the last time she was ever able to speak to them or hug them. Life is so precious. It is important to cherish every minute with our loved ones.

Relationships with other people can be one of the most rewarding or frustrating aspects of life, depending on our own reactions. Anytime two people come in contact with one other, the potential exists for synergy or conflict. The potential for synergy or conflict is related to your reactions to other people's behavior. We can only control our own reactions. We can never control other people's behavior. Therefore, the determining factor of your success and happiness is in your ability to be honest and authentic with a genuine desire to resolve problems collaboratively and creatively.

Forget about the wrong things people do to you. Don't try to get even. Love your neighbor as yourself. — Leviticus 19:18 (ERV, 2012).

As you think about creating your ideal life, think about and write down how you want your relationships to be with your family, friends, boss (if you have one), coworkers, and employees. All people deserve to be treated fairly, honestly, with respect, and dignity. We learned everything we needed to know about relationships in kindergarten.

Do for others what you would want them to do for you. — Matthew 7:12 (ERV, 2012)

As you think about your relationships, remember the part you play. Are you a good listener, or do you talk over other people? Do you expect more from them than you are willing to give? Are you flexible or rigid in your viewpoints? Are you accountable? Do you hold others accountable? One of the most important aspects of healthy relationships is communication, and the most important aspect of communication is listening. Do you seek to understand before you seek to be understood? People will open up to you and it will improve your relationships immensely when you stop focusing on what you want, and start focusing on what others need. Only when you have changed your mindset to focus on others will you have the healthy relationships you desire.

Other keys to healthy relationships that should go without saying include telling the truth and doing what you say you will do. Treat others with the same respect you desire, and you will find your relationships improving. Finally, take responsibility for your actions. If you hurt another person, whether it is intentional (I hope not), or accidental, take responsibility to apologize first and make it right immediately. Do not let open wounds fester for long. The best advice I ever received was never to go to bed angry. That advice works for all of your important relationships. Take a few minutes now and capture your vision for your relationships pillar in your workbook.

SERVICE

Don't aim at success - the more you aim at it and make it a target, the more you are going to miss it. For success, like happiness, cannot be pursued; it must ensue, and it only does so as the unintended side-effect of one's dedication to a cause greater than oneself or as the by-product of one's surrender to a person other than oneself. — Viktor Frankl.

Service to others is the foundation of a meaningful life and one of the Pillars of your ideal life. We all need to feel as though we are making a difference in the world. Your service may be to your family, your faith, your community, or to a charity. It may be part of what you do for a living. It may be how you interact with your employees as a servant leader. Again, here the focus is on other people and not on you. Your purpose will lead to your service. For example, perhaps your purpose as a mother is to raise healthy children who become good citizens and who lead happy lives. Your service, then, is to your children and to the greater good of the community. Does that make sense?

As a manager, your service may be to help your employees achieve their potential through coaching and teaching them. As an employee, your service may be to perform your job to the best of your ability, which in turn helps the company serve its customers better.

I don't remember where I read it, but I heard a story one time about two men who worked for a garbage-collection company. They performed the dirtiest job of all, which was riding on the back of the truck to pick up and empty the trashcans into the truck. At a company event one day, someone asked the men what they did for the company. One of the men said, "I empty the stinking trash cans into the truck." The other man said, "I help keep my community clean and beautiful." Each of the men performed the exact same job, but their mindsets and viewpoints were completely different. One was clearly focused on service; the other was focused on himself. Which of these two men do you identify with? Are you emptying the stinking trashcans or making your community beautiful?

Today, my service is in helping others achieve their ideal life. When I left my corporate job to purchase a business-coaching franchise, I found joy in helping small business owners. I formed strong connections with the entrepreneurs, professionals, and business owners who were passionate about their purpose. I believed in their dream, and I wanted to help them succeed. This is the secret of a strong purpose. People will line up to help you when they believe in your cause. Articulating a worthwhile purpose will energize you and inspire others to join you on your mission.

Pastor Rick Warren, in his book, *The Purpose Driven Life*, reminds us that our purpose is born of God. God purposefully placed you and me on the earth with the right blend of strengths, talents, and skills to serve. If, as we are taught, God is everywhere—then God is in us, too. Because of this, all things are possible through Him and the possibilities are endless and unlimited by anyone or anything. The only limitations, then, are in our own minds. You have been placed on Earth to make a difference. The challenge is discovering your true purpose.

I have learned through my journey that true happiness comes from purposeful living. What you focus on makes all the difference. I believe that happiness is not found in a job, or a title, or money. Happiness is found in the belief that you are making a difference in the world through service to others, including your loved ones. Passion for your work is driven by your purpose. Purpose fuels extraordinary achievement. This is empowering. With God on your side, you are unstoppable!

Discovering your purpose can be a lifelong journey, or it can happen overnight. The need to do something significant is part of creating sustainable passion for your work. Whether you are finding purpose and meaning in existing work, or finding different work that is meaningful, you are the ultimate arbitrator of what is meaningful. Meaningful work, then, is an individual decision. Each person has a unique and different sense of what is meaningful. You must first decide—then you must do.

I had a client in Houston, a nurse practitioner, who also had her own business. My client's passion was working with hospice patients. I personally don't believe I would be very good in this career, but my client was one of the most caring and compassionate people I have ever met. In talking with her, I learned about her motivation. She told me, "I work with the very young and the very old who are the closest to God. They are the best witness to my work on earth. Perhaps they will whisper in the ear of Our Maker that I did my work well." Talk about a compelling purpose. She brought tears to my eyes when she expressed her dedication to her purpose in life.

Your work is meaningful when it is focused on service to God and others. It is never meaningful when it is focused only on you. Go ahead and craft the vision for your service pillar. Who are you serving? What is your purpose? If you do not feel that what you are doing is meaningful, perhaps you need to think about what you would find meaningful and write that down, or perhaps you need to reexamine your viewpoint.

SPIRITUALITY

*You have to grow from the inside out. None can teach you, none can make you spiritual. There is no other teacher but your own soul. —
Swami Vivekananda*

There is power in belief: belief in yourself and belief in a higher power. Your spiritual pillar is related to your belief in a higher power. What you believe or don't believe is between you and God (or the Universe, or whatever you believe in). If you are struggling with understanding your purpose in life, or looking for meaning, I suggest you look at your spiritual pillar to see if you could envision a closer relationship with God. When I consciously decided I wanted a closer relationship with God, things in my life became clearer for me. I set aside time every day, usually early in the morning, for meditation, Bible study, and prayer. I trust if you seek a more meaningful spiritual life you will find one. What is your vision for your spiritual life? Does your spiritual pillar include a closer relationship with a higher power? Go ahead and capture that now. I will wait.

GRATITUDE

Happiness cannot be traveled to, owned, earned, worn, or consumed. Happiness is the spiritual experience of living every minute with love, grace, and gratitude. — Denis Waitley

A life full of gratitude is a life of abundance. Showing appreciation to others for the little things they do will improve your relationships, and it will improve you. Looking for good in others is a positive way of improving your own mood. If you genuinely appreciate people, and tell them so, they will walk over hot coals to do more so you can appreciate them more. It is the little things that matter. I had a boss who would leave me a voice mail after hours, thanking me for something I had done that was part of my job. It was not required, but it was so nice to have the effort recognized. We all want to be appreciated, don't we?

When was the last time you said a genuine *thank you* to your spouse or your children? How about your boss or your coworkers? We all crave appreciation, so make it a point to show a little appreciation on a regular basis—especially to those you care about most. If someone goes out of their way to take the time to do something for you, the least you can say is, "Thank you." The most precious gift someone can give to you is his or her time. Don't take it for granted. Acknowledge it. Be appreciative.

While we are on the subject, be sure to appreciate yourself. When someone shows appreciation to you, believe you are worth it. Don't *poo poo* it. Breathe in the appreciation you are given, and learn to say, "You are welcome." Danielle Laporte says, *"The gratitude you receive is a reflection of your genius."* Practice appreciation of others, and watch it come back to you in the form of appreciation for you.

You should find ways to appreciate your customers and employees. Send a handwritten card. Imagine going to your mailbox and receiving a card you were not expecting, and opening it to find out it was someone you have done business with or that you work for just wanting to say, "Thank you." It is powerful, and it is the most effective way of keeping your customers or employees for life. Customers and employees like to be appreciated, too. Do not send an email, because it will not have the same effect. Now, think about your gratitude pillar, and jot down how you envision gratitude in your ideal life. It really is the little things that matter the most.

TIME

Time is what we want most, but what we use worst. — William Penn

On Friday, June 24, 1994, I was standing in the heat in downtown Houston, Texas along with 400,000 others, waiting on the start of a parade to honor the Houston Rocket's 1994 Championship team.

We waited and waited and waited...

I had slipped out of my office in one of the high-rise buildings, and taken my place in the crowd to see the once-in-a-lifetime parade opportunity.

We continued to wait....

Finally, an hour after the parade was scheduled to start, it began. The parade started one hour late, because it had to wait on Hakeem Olajuwon to arrive. Olajuwon was the star of the show, and the NBA finals most valuable player. No parade for the Houston Rockets could start without him.

So where was Olajuwon, and why did he keep us waiting in the heat in downtown Houston on a hot summer afternoon?

We waited because Olajuwon had his personal priorities straight. The parade was delayed an hour because Olajuwon had attended a prayer service, and could not get into downtown because of the crowds. The star of the show felt his greatest personal priority was to pray before being honored for his part in the championship team. I admired the man. He had his priorities straight. Perhaps, his success was due, in part, to his sense of priority and duty to God.

So, what are your priorities? How do you decide?

In their book, *The ONE Thing*, Gary Keller and Jay Papasan, tell us that we should set our priorities by asking only one focusing question. Keller and Papasan suggest that multitasking is a myth, and that all of us should become more attentive to the things that really matter. The way to become more focused is to ask a directing question to guide our life and our daily choices. The question we should ask ourselves is this, *"What's the one thing I can do such that by doing it everything else will be easier or unnecessary?"*

What is your ONE thing?

Your life is full of choices. You get to choose where to prioritize your time, and time is limited. Will you choose to spend time with your children, or will you choose to spend time working? At the end of your life, you will not wish you had gotten one more thing done. You'll wish you had attended the baseball game where your son hit his only home run. None of us can cheat time. Make sure the choices you make about how to spend your time are the ones that you will be happy to look back on at the end of your life. Make sure your priorities are straight. Make sure your ONE thing is THE one thing.

> *Time, not money, is your biggest asset in life. You need time to invest in relationships (with yourself and your family) or to chase your passion. "Think again" if you are still trading off time for money. Let your money work for you. You don't work for money. That is exactly what Financial Freedom is... — Manoi Arora, From the Rat Race to Financial Freedom*

Making a meaningful life consists of balance. Are your priorities in the right order? If we are so busy making a living that we forget to make a life, we will reach the end of our lives and wonder what happened to all the time. No one is promised tomorrow.

In the section on Relationships, I told you about my friend who lost her two sons less than two years ago in a freak automobile accident. My friend would surely admonish you to spend time with your family. I have another friend who recently lost her husband to a freak motorcycle accident. He went to work one day, and did not make it home. This can happen to any of us at any time. We are not guaranteed the next minute or the next hour. Time is precious. Let's not waste one minute of it.

How much of your time will be given to working? I had a business client who assured me that he had his family priorities straight. He left work every day at 5:00 p.m. and went home to spend time with his wife and children. After they all went to bed, he got up and spent another two or three hours working. On vacations, the family traveled out of the country to see family. My client would spend time during the day with family, and because of the time differences, he would spent nights working. He felt he had it all under control, and that his life was in balance. In reality, he was burning the candle at both ends. The body needs sleep to rejuvenate. I worried about how many years he was sacrificing from the end of his life, while he thought he was cheating time by working around the clock. As you envision the time pillar in your ideal life, think about how you will spend your time. Will you spend most of it working, playing, or making memories with your family and friends? Will you spend time on self-development? You truly get to choose, and now is the time to reflect on how you currently spend your time to see if a change is needed. Is the way you spend the time in your life balanced? The goal is for you to reach the end of your life and have no regrets about how your time was spent. Right now, jot down the vision for the time pillar of your ideal life. We all have the same 1440 minutes in a day, and once they are gone, we cannot get them back. What you do with your allotted 1440 minutes will make the difference in your life and in the lives of your loved ones.

CAREER/BUSINESS

You can only become accomplished at something you truly love. Don't make money your goal. Instead, pursue the things that you love doing, and do them so well, people can't take their eyes off of you. — Maya Angelou

I sat in a presentation from Logan Stout, the CEO of IDLife this past weekend. He outlined the three stages of life. Read through these, and think about which stage of life you are in.

Stage 1: *Fear* — You are fearful of moving forward. Your life is currently in a mess; you are struggling, but you are afraid of making any change. You are afraid of getting out of bed every morning.

Stage 2: *Comfortable* — You are doing okay. You are making enough money, have a nice home and cars, but feel there has got to be more to life. You have realized that you want more, and want to make a difference. You dread getting out of bed every morning.

Stage 3: *Absolute Joy and Freedom* — You cannot wait to get up every day, because you are so excited about what you get to do every day.

Which stage are you honestly in today? And what will it take to get you to Stage 3? More importantly, how would it feel to live a Stage-3 life?

The challenge for everyone is to choose a career or business that will provide a Stage-3 life. Wouldn't it be great to live a Stage-3 life? For example, if your vision includes traveling around the world, and if your desire is to own a business, your business idea should probably not be a fast-food restaurant, unless of course you have the means to buy one that already functions without the owner's daily presence. When considering this choice, please consider what you *truly* value. We waited until the end of this section to look at your career or business. I wanted you to reflect and think about the other areas of your life first, before thinking about your career. At the end of the day, you want a career or business that will support your chosen life. Your life should not have to support your career or business.

Your career or business should include that one thing that gives you joy. What drives you? What did you learn in the previous sections of this book about your preferences? I won't go back through those things here. What I would suggest is to envision for yourself what your career or business should look like and write that down for this pillar. Answer this question: what would you do for free, if both money and time were no object?

Imagine, for just a moment, that you have suddenly come into $10 million dollars. That is enough money that you should never have to "work" another day. Think very carefully before answering my next question. Given the scenario, where you no longer need to work for the money, would you stay at your current job?

Why or why not? Be honest with yourself.

The people who say they would stay at their current job are often already in a role or job where they feel their work has meaning and purpose. Congratulations, if this describes you. Perhaps you are already living a Stage-3 life.

On the other hand, if you are like many people, you would jump at the chance to do something else, perhaps anything else. If you find that you dream of doing something else, then stop dreaming and take action. Buying this book is a good first step. The first section was to help you gain an understanding of your current situation. This section has taken you through a process of creating a vision for your life. Your next step is to decide for yourself exactly what you really want in a job and career.

In his book, *The Reinvention of Work: New Vision for Livelihood for Our Time* (New York, NY: Harper Collins, 1995, 95), Matthew Fox says, *"We have a right to and a need for joy in our work."*

What is so much fun to do that you can hardly stand it?

The answer to these questions may provide insight into what your vision might look like. What does your work environment look like? Are you working outside, or inside in an office? Finally, what work would you like to do that would be meaningful? Are you working with other people? Are you working alone? Think about this, and jot down your vision for your career or business.

In his book, *The Advantage: Why Organizational Health Trumps Everything Else in Business*, Patrick Lencioni suggests that the single-greatest advantage any organization can achieve is organizational health, but also suggests that many organizations ignore this aspect of their business. As a potential employee or business owner, you should also be concerned with organizational health. Think about the characteristics you require in an organization, and what a compatible work environment would be for you.

As I have already mentioned earlier in this book, I discovered that I was unhappy in my career. I made a good salary, and had achieved everything I had wanted to achieve, but I was still not happy. I realized I needed a change. I have been through a few changes as a result. Today, I now live a Stage-3 life. Every day, I get to help people live the life they want to live. Through my writing, speaking, and teaching, I have been afforded the opportunity to love getting out of bed every day. Every day, I get to help people improve their lives. I get to help them design their ideal life. I have made the decision to make the changes in my life to have the life I truly want to live. I am not there yet, but I am on track with my 24-month plan to get there. How about you? Do you even have a plan?

THE BOTTOM LINE

Keep your dreams alive. Understand to achieve anything requires faith and belief in yourself, vision, hard work, determination, and dedication. Remember all things are possible for those who believe. — Gail Devers

The perfect career or business for you will blend your unique strengths, talents, interests, and priorities into an opportunity to pursue a worthwhile, meaningful purpose in a work environment that will fit your personality and style. What works for me will not work for you. That is why this book so far has been a process of self-discovery. After completing this chapter, you have had the opportunity to cast the vision for your life for all 8 Pillars of Your Ideal Life.

The bottom line is you get to decide what you want from your life. No one else can do this for you. Once you have decided, you have to act upon the discoveries you have made. You are accountable for your own happiness. You alone are responsible for creating the life you desire.

It is your life. You get to choose how you live it. You can live it on purpose or without purpose. If you have not already done so, be sure and spend some time in the personal-reflection section of this chapter, or with your companion workbook crafting a vision for each pillar of your ideal life.

Are you all in? How does your current life feel? If your life is not quite where you want it to be, take heart. The next chapter will walk you through a process to create the action plan to move forward, and create your ideal life.

PERSONAL REFLECTION

FEELING IS THE THING

How do you want to feel in your life?

Identify your vision for each of the 8 Pillars of Your Ideal Life. When you are deciding on your future, you must create a compelling picture of how you want your life to look. Answer the following questions. Don't skip this step. It is very important. Close your eyes, and imagine the end result for each Pillar. Paint a vivid picture in your mind before you write the answers. Your thoughts precede your actions. Your actions determine your future. Your future starts in your mind. It starts right here. If you can envision it—it will happen.

My vision for each of the 8 Pillars of my life is

1. Health (Exercise, Nutrition, Energy, Diet, Mind, Sleep, Habits)
2. Money (Financial fitness, Good credit, Debt, Cash flow, Your credit score, Profits, Part-time income to financial fitness)
3. Relationships (Family, Friends, Boss, Coworkers, Employees, Community)
4. Service (Church, Charity, Work, Others, Family)
5. Spirituality (Faith, Belief)
6. Gratitude (Life of Appreciation)
7. Time (Working, Playing, Relationships, Self-Improvement)
8. Career/Business (Meaningful work, New Business, New Career, New Job)

Now, please answer these questions honestly.

- How do I define success?
- How do I define happiness?
- My top dreams in life are....
- What careers would I consider if I had the opportunity?
- What did I dream of doing as a child?
- If money were no object, what would I do?
- What do I love so much I would do it for free?

ENVISION YOUR MOST COMPATIBLE WORK OR BUSINESS ENVIRONMENT

Look at these concepts; circle your preferences, and jot your answers to help you narrow down the type of work or business you prefer. These are meant to jog your thought process as you ponder your most compatible career or business. These questions are derived, in part, from those found in Nicolas Lore's, *The Pathfinder: How to Choose or Change Your Career for a Lifetime of Satisfaction and Success* (New York, NY: Simon and Schuster, 1998).

HUMAN ENVIRONMENT

- Are you out in front leading, or working in a supporting role?
- Are you interacting with other people, or working alone behind the scenes?
- Are you in daily contact with: customers, clients, fellow workers, employees, adults, or children?
- Are you working with: young people, the elderly, professionals, a particular profession, people in need, people seeking to make a purchase, people trying to solve a problem, people seeking to learn something, people from other cultures, people from a specific socioeconomic group?
- Are your fellow employees: professionals, technical, blue collar, creative, cooperative, young, highly motivated, etc.?
- Are you working in a team? What type of team?
- How much collaboration, versus independence, do you prefer?
- What style of supervision do you prefer?

GEOGRAPHICAL AND PHYSICAL ENVIRONMENT

- Are you living and working in an urban or rural environment? Or do you live in the suburbs and commute to the city every day?

- Are you working indoors or outdoors?
- Are you frequently traveling or limited to little or no travel?
- Are you sitting at a desk in a cubicle in an office building, or calling on clients outside the office, or something else?

ORGANIZATIONAL ENVIRONMENT

- Are you working for someone else or self-employed?
- Are you working in a large corporation, small company, or just you?
- Do you desire opportunities for advancement and public recognition?
- Are you content with making a meaningful contribution with private appreciation?
- Are you comfortable in an organization with political maneuvering and seniority considerations?
- Do you prefer a start-up company with growth potential or an established company with limited growth and more security?

NATURE OF THE WORK

- Does your work have someone else defining the objectives and providing a structured methodology to perform it?
- Does your work have someone else providing the big picture objectives and leaving it up to you to define the methodology?
- Is the pace fast, moderate, or slow?
- Are you busy all day or do you have slack time?
- Are you making decisions all day, every day, or only occasionally?
- Does the work require spur-of-the-moment decisions, or allow for meticulous, carefully planned decision-making?
- Do you know what you will face when you get to work every day, or do you enjoy not knowing what each day will bring?

- Does your preferred work environment have a continual stream of new projects, assignments, and problems, or provide a steady routine that does not vary much?
- Do you want your job to be challenging?
- Do you prefer comfort or adventure?
- Is it important to have fun at work?

PRIORITIES AND TIME SPENT AT WORK

- How much of your available time will be spent working? Include commuting, networking, work taken home, and time away from work spent thinking or worrying about work.
- Are you willing to respond to emergency calls and other special situations that may require you to give extra time and effort to your work?
- Is it important for you to have time available for hobbies, family, volunteering, and other outside activities?

SECURITY, PORTABILITY, AND RETIREMENT

- How much job security do you desire?
- How long do you plan to work? Do you plan to retire early, or keep working until you are no longer able to work?
- Do you want your career to be portable, so you can find a job easily on short notice anywhere?

WHAT ABOUT THE OTHER PEOPLE IN YOUR LIFE?

- Do other people in your life have plans that may impact your career choices?
- Are you planning to get married? Get divorced?
- In a two-career family, whose career will come first?

- Do you need to consider the care of small children or elderly parents?

REWARDS

- How do you want others to perceive your work?
- How much income and income potential? Now? In five years? Later on?
- What about other financial incentives? Bonuses? Stock options? Company car?
- Are you interested in partnership or partial ownership?
- Do you desire recognition or appreciation for your work?

POWER AND STATUS

- How important are power and status to you?
- Do you desire fame or public recognition?
- Is it important for your work to be known outside your immediate group'?
- Do you crave respect and admiration from others?
- Do you desire to achieve status (at work, in your profession, in the community)?

BENEVOLENCE AND SOCIAL RESPONSIBILITY

- Do you desire to make an important impact to humanity?
- On which groups do you desire to make an impact? What sort of impact?
- Do you want your work to directly make a contribution, or is it sufficient that you work for an organization that does something you care about or believe in?

WRAPPING IT UP

Go back through this section and ask yourself, "What am I sure will be an important aspect of my future career or business?" Add these to your list.

Based on what you have learned from this exercise, describe in a short paragraph your most ideal career and work environment.

Did you close your eyes and really think about it? How did it feel? Please don't move on to the next chapter until you have written down your vision for each of the 8 Pillars of Your Ideal Life.

CHAPTER SIX: DESIGN YOUR ACTION PLAN

TIME TO TAKE ACTION

It is now time to take action. In the previous chapters of this book, you have worked through a process to understand your strengths and to cast your vision for your ideal life. Close your eyes for one more time, and think deeply about that vision. How did it feel? Feels good, right?

You now have a dream, but do you have a workable plan? If you stop at this point, you will have a wish, but you will not have a plan. The first key to having the life you desire is to write down what you want with manageable, trackable goals. Follow along with me here to create your plan. The time is NOW to take action on your future.

Dreams remain dreams without goals. — Denzel Washington

To achieve success and happiness, you must get crystal clear on what you want and why. Our lives are about the choices we make. You will always have too many things to do, and too little time to do them. Achievement starts with establishing goals for important wants and desires. You must set priorities among competing demands. Concentrate your energy and focus on high-priority high-value activities—those that move you closer to your vision. With a clear focus on what you want, you can do less and achieve more. You will be tackling things that matter the most to you. Ask yourself the focusing question: what is the ONE thing you can do next to take you toward your dreams?

Following Stephen Covey's advice, *"Begin with the end in mind,"* I set goals by starting with what I want to achieve in a given timeframe.

From your vision, spend a few minutes with your workbook, and jot down the steps you can think about right now that are needed to achieve what you want. For example, if your vision includes a career change, what are the skills you will need to attain? Do you need to return to school? Do you need to talk to someone who has that career to learn more? If you are considering starting a business, do you need to talk to the SCORE advisors at your local Small Business Development Center?

For example, when I left my coaching business, I decided that I wanted to teach at the college level for my "retirement." I need an advanced degree to do that, so I searched for a program that fit my interests. I researched the schools that offered that program. I verified the availability of financial aid. I applied to the program. I was accepted. See how this works? I started with the end goal of becoming a University instructor in seven years, and worked my way backward to what I needed to accomplish short-term to get there. On a daily basis, I evaluate what I need to do to take a step closer to that goal. That could be something as simple as finishing my assignment, or posting my required response on the online forum.

Here are the steps you can take toward your vision:

- Review your long-term vision, and break it down into shorter manageable steps.
- Create and write down SMART goals. SMART Goals are Specific, Measurable, Attainable, Relevant, and Time-based.
- Start each week by reviewing your SMART goals. Set your priorities for the week based on what you need to accomplish. Do not let outside distractions derail your plans.
- Identify the most important actions to take to achieve each of your goals.
- Block time to do them. And do them.
- Create goals that are congruent with the values and vision you described in previous sections of this book.

Do this, and you will naturally feel energized, motivated, and inspired to take action daily on your goals. Focus on the vital few things—not the trivial many. Set big goals—goals on steroids.

Articulating your goals using the SMART formula creates a specificity that harnesses the powerful, cybernetic, goal-seeking ability within each of us.

For instance, if one of your SMART goals is to write a book, you might say "I will write just two pages a day of rough copy, without editing, for 90 days; I will have my 180-page first draft in my hands by (insert a date three months from now)." This goal is specific, measurable, attainable, relevant, and time-based. You can track whether you have attained it, and you can hold yourself accountable (or ask someone else to).

When going through the goal-setting process, brainstorm both personal and professional goals. The list in the personal-reflection section of this chapter touches on some areas of your life to consider as you brainstorm your list of goals. You do not have to write a goal for every area, just use the list as a memory jogger. Stop here, and go brainstorm your list of goals in your workbook.

Go big....dream big....

THE POWER OF FOCUS

Now that you have brainstormed and written down your goals, it is time to focus and prioritize. Trying to do too much is just as unproductive as trying to do too little. Focus your energy on the activities that will bring you the most joy and success.

Go through your list, and pick the top seven goals that will take you closer to the dreams you have. Pick the seven that you can achieve in 90 days or less. If the goals will take longer than 90 days, break them down into steps that can be managed in 90 days. Let's say your long-term goal is to go back to school and get another degree so you can change careers. Perhaps in the next 90 days, you can realistically evaluate and select a college program in which to enroll. Or perhaps your goal is to start a new business. In the next 90 days, you can realistically evaluate some possible business opportunities, or you could schedule an appointment to speak to a SCORE advisor. The point is to take action toward your long-term desires.

- Write down your top seven goals. Make sure they are SMART goals. Remember, SMART Goals are Specific, Measurable, Attainable, Relevant, and Time-based.
- Make a commitment to complete these seven goals in 90 days or less.

Denis Waitley suggests a 90-day cycle for success:

Your 90-day season of success will build your motivation because, often, yearly or five-year goals are so distant that it's easy to get discouraged and give up on them in frustration. When your goals are proximate and positively pressing, you're more likely to muster the motivation necessary to achieve them.

Once you have written down your top seven quarterly goals, put them in a place where you can review them every day. Focusing on your goals daily will help you prioritize your daily activities. Review your top seven goals every 90 days—evaluate how well you did, and what is left to do. Go through this process and reset and refocus....

People who achieve extraordinary results in life and business use a system like I've just taught you. And they do one other thing: they take action immediately.

Start right now by going to the personal-reflection section for this chapter in your workbook to create your 90-day SMART goals and action plan.

TAKE PRIORITIZED ACTION DAILY

You have now gone through the process of creating your vision and goals for every area of your life. You have narrowed down your goals to the top seven that you will accomplish in the next 90 days. The next step is to take those 90-day goals to create action every day.

To be more productive, you need a priority-management system that you can trust to keep up with the actionable items and reference materials that you need. This can be paper-based or electronic—it is just a tool to facilitate the day-to-day choices you need to make on how to allocate your time.

Getting the stuff out of your head and into a system you trust will free your mind to focus on your priorities. Following a consistent and disciplined time-organization process should increase your productivity from 30 – 70%.

David Allen, the author of *Getting Things Done* outlines a system for prioritizing daily activities. Time management is a myth. You can only better prioritize the time you do have. If organization is one of your challenges, I highly recommend you get David Allen's book and review his website for additional tools to help you.

PRIORITY MANAGEMENT SYSTEM

Every priority-management system requires these items: goals, calendar, contact management, notes and documents, and to-do list.

CALENDAR

- Have only one calendar to work from – paper-based or electronic
- Only plan 60 - 70% of your day – to allow for the inevitable interruptions that will occur
- Your calendar must be portable so you can carry it with you
- Keep your calendar updated regularly to manage deadlines and meetings
- New items should be added immediately so they are not forgotten

TO DO LISTS

- Keep two task lists – Master To Do List and Must Do Today List
- Everything personal and professionally that needs to be done must go on the Master To Do List
- Include the date each item is due
- Must Do Today List contains the three to five things you must do today
- Estimate how long each item will take—then schedule them on your calendar
- Set aside blocks of time to focus on important tasks

TO DON'T LIST

- Almost as important as the things you will do are the things you will stop doing. Make your commitments today.
- Create your To Don't list—write down the list of things you will not do, or that you will stop doing.

CONTACT MANAGEMENT

- Contact Management is a critical strategy for effective time prioritization
- The average business person may spend anywhere from 30 to 60 minutes per day looking for contact information
- Your contact management system can be kept electronically or on paper
- Keeping your contact information electronically allows you to leverage the information for various purposes
- Select a contact-management system and stick with it
- Put all of your contacts, both professional and personal, in one system
- Your contact-management system needs to be portable so you can carry it with you at all times
- You can never be sure when you might need to find a phone number to touch base with a client, call a prospect, or give a referral.

NOTES

- Keeping good notes will allow you to recall what was discussed, what was agreed to, and what your action-items are related to your clients, your organization, your prospects, and your referral partners.
- Note-keeping can be electronic or paper-based

- Effective note-taking requires doing it consistently and managing them once they have been captured
- Review notes daily to add action items to your Master To Do List

MANAGING EMAIL

- Set aside time two or three times per day to manage email
- Turn off email notifications to minimize distractions so you can focus on higher value activities throughout the day
- Make a point to empty your inbox every day
- Try to avoid handling an email more than twice
- Respond to emails requiring an immediate response
- Complete any actions that you can complete in under two minutes
- Delete emails you don't need to keep
- File emails you do need to keep
- Organize actions and follow-up items
    - Greater than two minutes to do
    - Waiting on someone else to do
- Keep your actionable and non-actionable emails in separate places

PERSONAL INVENTORY CONTROL

- Keep and use legal pads and pens wherever you work, think, or communicate
- Take notes while you listen, think, and talk
- Organize your action items, projects, references, and support materials
- Keep lists to group similar things (all your errands, calls, etc.) plus use a filing system for project notes.
- Review your lists of action items and projects regularly enough to trust you will not miss anything

- At least once a week, review all projects you are committed to finishing, and determine what action you need to take on each one.

WEEKLY REVIEW

- Schedule time on your calendar to do a weekly review
- Process all outstanding materials, meeting notes, voice mails, emails
- Empty your head—capture new projects, actions, ideas, and items that are "waiting for" something
- Review action lists—mark completed items
- Review past week's calendar dates to capture remaining action items, reference data, or appointments—transfer these into your working system
- Review upcoming calendar—capture any actions
- Determine if there are any impending deadlines (e.g. proposals due, or commitments)
- Review list of "waiting for" items—check off received ones
- Evaluate status of projects, goals, and outcomes
- Review any relevant checklists
- Create To Do's on the appropriate To Do List for each day
- Block time on your calendar for phone calls, emails, administrative work, etc.
- Review accomplishments associated with goals
- Allocate time on your calendar for important activities

DAILY

- Review your 90-day goals for anything you need to do today
- Review all appointments for today and this week—schedule time for preparation

- Review Master To Do List and create Must Do Today List for the day
- Review your Must Do Today List and estimate the time needed for each task
- Schedule time on your calendar during the day to complete the tasks
- Determine your three most important activities and desired outcomes for the day
- Say positive affirmations to set your mindset for the day

Taking this systematized approach to planning each day will help you break your 90-day goals down into focused, daily action. Remember, all you have to do is take one step a day to get closer to your dreams. Many people give up because they lose focus. When they lose focus, other things get in the way. Don't wake up in two years and find out you have accomplished nothing on the dreams you have worked on in this book. Take my advice, and follow this simple daily process. You will achieve massive results.

THE POWER OF PART TIME

You may be thinking at this point that you just don't have the time to work on your dreams. You have a family and a full-time job. You have other commitments. I get that. So do I. You have the ability to work on your dream part-time. I wrote this book part-time while holding down a full-time job, going to graduate school, and working on two part-time businesses. I established a goal, after *Share Your Message With The World* was published, to finish the first draft of this book by September 3, 2014 and to get it into the hands of my good friend, Dennis Welch. I did not hit that date, but I was close. I was able to get there by shooting for the goal, and by taking a few steps every day. Some days, I only wrote a few paragraphs, but I was able to make progress. Make sure you prioritize the things that matter most to you—then just do them.

My number-one desire is to achieve freedom. Freedom for me includes freedom from debt and freedom of time to spend with my friends and family. I got tired of being overweight, and out of energy, and not sleeping each night. I also got tired of feeling trapped by my debt and other obligations. The feeling of being trapped spilled over into my personal relationships. It was not pretty. I started my part-time businesses to work toward both better personal and financial health. I am happy to say I am on track to pay off my debt in two years; in three years, I will have the residual income from my part-time businesses to replace my full-time job. Jim Rohn, America's Philosopher says, "*Profits are better than wages.*" This is true from many standpoints, including the tax advantages and the other advantages of owning a business and not having a 9:00 a.m. to 5:00 p.m. J-O-B.

My part-time businesses provide me with the vehicle to achieve my goals, and to help so many other people achieve their goals. They are the perfect opportunity for me, at the perfect time, to make a significant difference in the lives of many others.

You have to decide what is important to you. Then, start part-time to make it happen. If I can do it, you can too.

YOUR MINDSET

Most people can do anything they choose to do. The problem is that many don't believe they *can* do it. They give up before they ever really try. The border bullies get in the way of them truly getting what they want. Negative self-talk should be flushed down the toilet. If you don't fill your mind with positive talk, it will fill itself with doubts and disbelief. Your mind is powerful. As we have already learned, our thoughts precede our actions. If we believe it—we can do it.

This has not always been easy for me—and in fact, I still struggle. I absolutely hate using the phone to call prospects or for follow-ups. You may remember that I gave up my coaching business because I hated chasing people for money. But, I must do these things to have the freedom I desire. My *why* is bigger than my *fear*. Is your why bigger than your fear?

I do two things to conquer fear. I spend a lot of time and money on personal development. I cannot change my life if I don't change me. I find every opportunity to feed myself positive information. I listen to audios, read books, and attend seminars. I attend every live event and webinar I can squeeze in to make sure I am working constantly on my mindset. The second thing I do when I am not engaged in personal development is to use affirmations. I have little signs taped to my computer monitor. The one I am looking at right now says, INSPIRE FREEDOM! I give myself positive affirmations every day. My affirmations are stated in the positive, and always start with "I am...." I am helping people achieve their dreams. I am worthy of an awesome life. I am a best selling author. I am....

You get the idea. You should sit down and come up with about ten to 12 affirmations for yourself. You should read them out loud every morning when you get up, and every evening when you go to bed. Your brain will get the message. And when you can think it, and you truly believe it—you can do it. Guaranteed.

PERSONAL REFLECTION

Think about your vision as you go through each of these areas of your personal and professional life. Go ahead and jot down any goals that come to mind. We will come back and refine them later.

PROFESSIONAL GOALS

- Financial
- Staff development
- Leadership
- Systems
- Operational
- Public relations
- Employee management
- Strategic plans
- Technology
- Freedom
- Balance
- Income
- Priority management
- Career
- Other

PERSONAL GOALS

- Financial
- Health
- Family/marriage
- Mental/educational/skills/knowledge
- Fun/play/social
- Character
- Toy/possession
- Spiritual

Now that you have a good list, go back through and pick out the top seven goals you want to focus on for the next 90 days. Add them as SMART Goals in the table below.

WHAT IS THE GOAL?	WHOSE HELP DO I NEED?	BY WHEN?
1.		
2.		
3.		
4.		
5.		
6.		
7.		

Write your commitment here to complete these seven goals in the next 90 days. (90 days from today is: _____).

Now, print your goals out or copy them onto a piece of paper that you can put somewhere so you will look at them every day. Make them into a screen saver for your computer. Put them on your phone. Whatever you need to do to make sure you see them every day. Why, you may ask? When Napoleon Hill sought out the advice of the richest men in the world, they gave him the two secrets of their success. Do you remember what they were? The first secret was to write down your goals. You have just done that. The second secret was to look at them everyday. If it was good enough for the richest men in the world, it should be good enough for you.

Now that you have your goals, you need to translate those into daily and weekly actions.

Write out your ten to 12 affirmations, and read them out loud each morning when you get up and each evening right before bed.

When you have completed these activities, you are ready to move forward to create your ideal life.

CHAPTER SEVEN: DO YOUR DESTINY

GET OFF THE COUCH

Action is the foundational key to all success. — *Pablo Picasso*

For this book—or any self-improvement program—to benefit you, you must take action. Ideas only become reality when you take action to achieve them. You cannot read about becoming a surgeon, and expect to perform surgery. You have to obtain the knowledge, training, and practice to perform. Any worthwhile undertaking, including a career change or starting a new business, demands the same.

The more alignment you have between the inner and outer you, the more creative energy will motivate and inspire you. When you are in alignment with your purpose, you will more easily attract what you want and need. But none of this happens magically.

To find happiness and success, you must take action!

Using what you have learned about yourself from this book, you now have a powerful understanding of the things that truly matter most to you. You have created a personal and professional vision. You have sorted through your strengths, talents, and desires. You have faced your FUDS. You have taken a hard look at your most compatible work environment. You stood up to your border bullies.

You are now armed for the next steps in your journey.

The exercises in the personal-reflection sections of this book thus far have helped you gain clarity about yourself and what you really want. They have helped you focus on designing a vision for your desired future. You have created a focused set of 90-day SMART goals, and you now have a powerful system for prioritizing your activities. But, clarity and focus are not quite enough to create success and happiness. In addition to clarity and focus, you must add drive and accountability.

Your next steps are to focus on your goals and take action. You will have to get off the couch to have the life you desire.

ACT NOW!

Focused action is the secret behind the information I am sharing with you.

ACCOUNTABILITY

I almost did not put this section in the book. Many people cringe at the word "accountability." Why is accountability viewed so negatively? I think it is because people do not want to feel coerced into doing something they don't really want to do. Neither do I. But, in this case, a dose of accountability may be the one thing that helps you stay on track with your dreams and your goals. After all, we have already said that life will get in the way. Who will help keep you on track? Have you shared your dreams with someone else? Does your spouse or significant other support your dreams? Will they help you stay on track?

I find it interesting that we are often afraid to share our innermost dreams with those we love. Often, I think we are just afraid of what they will think or say. Our well-meaning family and friends may not understand us. They may say something unintentionally that crushes that little fire that burns within us. They do not mean to do it. They actually think they are "helping." If you are able to share your dreams with your loved ones, by all means you should do so. Get them on board. They can help you by providing encouragement and support.

If you are not quite ready to share your dream with your family that is all right, too, but do not let yourself off the hook. You need to share with someone who can help hold you accountable. Tell a friend, find an accountability partner, hire a coach, or join a mastermind group. Do something to help keep you on track.

Part of accountability is to write down your goals as discussed earlier in this book. Writing them down and looking at them will help keep you focused and on track. Sharing your goals with someone else is also a powerful motivator to stay on track. Saying them out loud helps make them real. Telling someone else, and asking that person to help hold you accountable, can keep you focused. It is too easy to procrastinate on something if no one else knows about it. It is easy to make excuses to ourselves. It is harder to make excuses to someone else. If your spouse knows you have committed to writing for one hour each morning, perhaps they will help you find the space and time to do so. If they don't know about the commitment you have made to yourself, they will "help you" find other activities to fill your time.

Once you start the 90-day goal process, you are instilling lifelong habits that will help change your life. Don't forget to repeat the process every 90-days. Look at your previous goals, note which ones you attained, and which are left undone. Celebrate the goals you accomplished. Determine if the undone goals are still a priority. If they are, write them down and give yourself a new due date. If they are not, throw them out and set new goals. This is an ongoing process of moving toward your dreams. Your accountability partner or coach can help you stay on track with this. Sustaining the changes you are making will be worthwhile, but will also require your conscious effort.

I don't like the word "accountability" either. I prefer to think of accountability as personal integrity. To me, integrity means doing what I say I will do. If I tell someone I am going to do something, I will do it. If something comes up, I don't make excuses. I apologize, and accept the consequences. I alone am accountable for my own results. If I don't make it happen, it won't happen. This is why having an accountability partner or coach is so powerful. If I tell someone else I am going to do something, I am determined not to let that person down. After all, if I do, my integrity is at stake.

In an earlier section in this book, I declared out loud to you, my readers, some of my business and financial goals. You can be sure I will be working hard to make sure I don't let you, or myself down. So, as you move forward toward your dreams, find someone who can help hold you accountable. Your accountability partner will help you stay focused on the dreams and goals you have set for yourself. If you are not willing to be held accountable to your own dreams, then perhaps you just don't want it badly enough. How about it?

DRIVE

The one thing that highly successful people do that other people don't do is continually drive toward their goals. This is not to say they don't get sidetracked, after all, life does happen along the way. What successful people are able to do is to notice when they are off track, and refocus their efforts toward what truly matters.

Drive means that you are in a constant state of action. When others are sleeping, you are up an hour early, writing a few paragraphs for your book. When others are watching television, you are reading and preparing yourself for your next challenge. When others are playing video games, you are thinking about what needs to be accomplished tomorrow and next week, and making your plans. You make conscious choices that take you closer to your dreams and spend what little time you have wisely. You find ways to overcome the obstacles that will present themselves and sometimes, you just have to get out of your own way to move forward.

For me, drive means having a laser-like focus on what success and happiness mean to me and continually refocusing on what is important. Over time, I have gained clarity around what I really want to achieve. My focus is on freedom. Freedom means time. Money provides freedom. The actions I take today are focused on a long-term goal of freedom. Time freedom. Financial freedom. That focus propels me toward action. Along the way, I get to help others achieve their goals. I am truly blessed to have the opportunity to do something I love, and help others do the same.

I am writing this book to help you achieve your ideal life, but just reading this book will not make you successful or happy. You have to focus on what matters most to you, and take action. The hardest step you will ever take is this: **Gain clarity about what you really want, and know what will truly make you happy**. Once you have clarity, you can focus on your goals and drive forward with action. The good news is if you have done the work in the first part of this book to gain clarity, you are miles ahead of 95% of the people in the world who are just drifting along aimlessly, hoping and wishing for a miracle, or to win the lottery. The real miracle is that you now know what you want, and you have a plan to get there. So what's next?

LIFE AFTER ACTION

Remember the time will pass whether you take action or not. You can choose to take action, or you can choose to sit out.

I alluded earlier in the book about the importance of learning. Personal development and education have been key contributors to my success. I urge you not to stop with this book. If you don't feel you have time to read, then buy books on audio, and listen to them in your car. Your university on wheels can help you continue to grow and wisely utilize wasted commute time. Learning also includes figuring out what works for you, and what does not work. That means, you will make mistakes. The key is to learn from the mistake, course correct, and move on. Our growth comes from stepping outside of our comfort zones. Sometimes, you will succeed...sometimes, you won't. It is part of learning and living. Failure is not the end of the world. It merely takes you one step closer to success.

Failure is not fatal, but failure to change might be. — John Wooden

As you move toward your dreams and goals, reach back to help others who are not as far along the path as you are. That is partly the reason for this book. I am still working on my goals—my life is a work in progress, but I know that I am blessed and can help others who are struggling to figure things out. Helping others gives me joy.

Happiness occurs naturally when your success is based on serving others with passion. Imagine how it would feel to spring out of bed every morning excited about the prospect of facing a new day. This is the new reality for a person on a purpose-driven mission. You cannot wait to talk to your clients or employees. You are happy and excited to be contributing and serving using your God-given talents.

It may seem overwhelming to think that you have to start over again, or that you need to go back to school for a couple of years to make the change you want to make. Change of any kind can be scary. If you don't make the change now, where will you be in two years? Or five years?

When you follow your passion, after discovering the one thing that you are meant to do, your life suddenly takes on new meaning. You will spring out of bed every morning excited to see what will happen. Your life will be filled with joy. Your positive outlook will bring positive people into your life. Your joy will create joy in the lives of others. Your significant relationships will improve.

The benefits of following your passion to do meaningful work are significant.

Studies have shown meaningfulness is positively related to psychological well-being, positive mood, psychological benefits, intrinsic work-satisfaction, and job involvement. Work passion has been shown to be positively related to improved work performance, psychological well-being, concentration, affective commitment, autotelic experience, sense of control, vitality, and engagement. As you can see, studies show that following our passions to do meaningful work is a powerful force in our lives.

PERSONAL REFLECTION

If you have worked through the personal reflections in this book, you now have a vision and goals. If you have not worked them yet, I urge you go back and work through them. The power of this book is in the work you put in on yourself and your dreams. Your next step is to take action. Jot down here the one activity you will do within the next 24 hours to take action. Then do it like your life depends upon it—because it does.

CHAPTER EIGHT: CONCLUSION

CONCLUSION

I hope you have found this book to be helpful, and that it will benefit you as you continue on your journey. You have worked hard on designing the life of your dreams. You now have a powerful process you can use at anytime to change the course of your life.

Just think. As a result of working through this book, you have clarity about what you really want in life. You have a powerful and important purpose. You are focused and effective. You are happier. Your family is happier. But more importantly, you are making a significant difference in the world. You are in harmony with the universe. The result is an amazing calm and peace.

You are doing the one thing you are meant to do, and making a difference in the world! How awesome is that?

Whether that is your current reality or your vision for the future, my wish for you is abundant success and happiness. Armed with knowledge about yourself, a compelling vision, your goals, and the courage to take action, you are destined to succeed and be happy.

Your journey—your happiness—your success story…*you* are the reason I wrote this book. I would love to hear from you.

CHAPTER NINE: RESOURCES

TOOLS OF SELF DISCOVERY

In addition to the self-exploration exercises in this book, our website is updated regularly with the latest in resources, tools, and assessments. Check them out at http://DesigningYourIdealLife.com.

The access code is BLUEPRINT.

ASSESSMENTS

Clifton Strengths Finder: https://www.gallupstrengthscenter.com

DISC Profile: To take a free online DISC assessment, visit PeopleKeys https://free.peoplekeys.com

Motivation Scale: From Tamara Lowe's, Get Motivated. http://www.motivatedbythebook.com

Myers Briggs: http://www.myersbriggs.org

Personality Tests: A collection of interactive personality tests, including an open-source DISC assessment, is located at this site http://www.personality-testing.info

Risk Tolerance Quiz: http://www.bankrate.com/brm/news/investing/20011127a.asp

BOOKS

Finding Work When There Are No Jobs by Roger Wright

Getting Things Done by David Allen

The Advantage by Patrick Lencioni

The ONE Thing by Gary Keller and Jay Papasan

The Pathfinder by Nicholas Lore

ADDITIONAL RESOURCES

Go to our website at http://www.DesigningYourIdealLife.com to sign up, download the companion workbook, and find other resources and bonus materials to accompany this book. The access code is BLUEPRINT. You will be able to follow along and work the exercises from the personal-reflection sections at the end of each chapter directly in your own ideal life workbook.

Also at our website, http://DesigningYourIdealLife.com you will find additional resources to help you design your ideal life.

- Find helpful resources
- Sign up for our online community
- Join a mastermind group
- Find an accountability partner
- Sign up for online training
- Take online assessments
- Find additional resources and tools
- Inquire about our consulting or coaching services
- Book us for a speaking engagement
- Leave us a comment about the book

If you wish to learn more about IDLife, you can do so at http://myIDLifeForce.com. While you are there, feel free to take the free personalized IDNutrition assessment.

REFERENCES

Albrecht, Simon L. "Work Engagement and the Positive Power of Meaningful Work." *Advances in Positive Organizational Psychology* 1 (2013): 237-260.

Allen, David. *Getting Things Done: The Art of Stress-free Productivity*. New York: Penguin, 2002.

Andersen, Wayne S. *Dr. A's Habits of Health: The Path to Permanent Weight Control & Optimal Health*. Annapolis, MD: Habits of Health Press, 2008.

Bonnstetter, Bill J., and Judy I. Suiter. *The Universal Language, DISC: A Reference Manual*. Phoenix: Target Training International, 2004.

Boverie, Patricia Eileen, and Michael S. Kroth. *Transforming Work: The Five Keys to Achieving Trust, Commitment, and Passion in the Workplace*. Cambridge, MA: Perseus Publishing, 2001.

Canfield, Jack, and Janet Switzer. *The Success Principles: How to Get From Where You Are to Where You Want to Be*. New York, NY: Harper Collins, 2007.

Cathcart, Jim. *The Acorn Principle: Know Yourself— Grow Yourself*. New York, NY: St. Martin's Press, 1998, 95-110.

Covey, Stephen R., A. Roger Merrill, and Rebecca R. Merrill. *First Things First*. New York: Simon and Schuster, 1995.

Ellis, Linda, and Mac Anderson. *The Dash: Making a Difference with Your Life from Beginning to End*. Nashville, TN: Thomas Nelson, 2012.

Fox, Matthew. *The Reinvention of Work: New Vision for Livelihood for Our Time*. New York, NY: Harper Collins, 1995.

Frankl, Viktor. E. *Man's Search for Meaning*. Boston: Beacon Press, 1959.

Hill, Napoleon. *Think and Grow Rich*. Meriden, CT: The Ralston Society, 1937.

Jones, Cathleen S., and Nell T. Hartley. "Comparing Correlations Between Four-Quadrant And Five-Factor Personality Assessments." *American Journal of Business Education (AJBE)* 6, no. 4 (2013): 459-470.

Kahn, William A. "Psychological Conditions of Personal Engagement and Disengagement at Work."*Academy of Management Journal 33,* no. 4 (1990): 692-724.

Kahn, William A. "To be Fully There: Psychological Presence at Work.*" Human Relations 45,* no. 4 (1992): 321-349.

Kiyosaki, Robert T., and Sharon L. Lechter. *Rich Dad's Cashflow Quadrant: Rich Dad's Guide to Financial Freedom.* New York, NY: Warner Books, 1999.

LaPorte, Danielle. *The Fire Starter Sessions: A Soulful + Practical Guide to Creating Success on Your Own Terms.* New York, NY: Crown Publishing, 2012.

Lencioni, Patrick. *The Advantage: Why Organizational Health Trumps Everything Else in Business.* San Francisco, CA: Jossey-Bass, 2012.

Lore, Nicholas. *The Pathfinder: How to Choose or Change Your Career for a Lifetime of Satisfaction and Success.* New York, NY: Simon and Schuster, 1998.

Luft, Joseph., and Harrington Ingham. "The Johari Window, a Graphic Model of Interpersonal Awareness." In Proceedings of the Western Training Laboratory in Group Development. Los Angeles, CA: UCLA, 1955.

Luft, Joseph. *Of Human Interaction.* Palo Alto, CA: National Press, 1969, 177.

Marston, William Moulton. *Emotions of Normal People.* New York: Harcourt Brace, 1928.

May, D. R., Gilson, R. L., & Harter, L. M. (2004). "The Psychological Conditions of Meaningfulness, Safety and Availability and the Engagement of the Human Spirit at Work." *Journal of Occupational and Organizational Psychology, 77,* 11-37.

Mendelson, Sidney. *Everything Counts, Everyone Matters: The Source for Sales, Relationship Management & Life Success.* Sidney Mendelson Publisher, 2010.

Ortberg, John. *When the Game Is Over, It All Goes Back in the Box.* Grand Rapids, MI: Zondervan, 2007.

"Pillar." *Merriam-Webster.com*. Accessed August 4, 2014. http://www.merriam-webster.com/dictionary/pillar.

Rohn, Jim. *Building Your Network Marketing Business (Audio)*. Jim Rohn International, 2010.

Sinetar, Marsha. *Do What You Love, The Money Will Follow*. New York, NY: Dell Publishing, 1987.

Smith, Becky Lynn. "Escaping Success to Find Happiness." in *Share Your Message with the World*, compiled by Tony Gambone, 113-118. London, UK: CM Publisher, 2014.

Tartakovsky, Margarita. "7 Mistaken Beliefs About Money." *Psych Central*, 2013. Accessed August 6, 2014, http://psychcentral.com/blog/archives/2013/04/09/7-mistaken-beliefs-about-money/

The Gallup Organization. *State of the American Workplace*. Washington, DC: Gallup, 2013.

The Institute for Motivational Living, Inc. "The Trust Model Adapted from the Johari Window." *Introduction to Behavioral Analysis Online Course Certification Guide*, 2011, 6.

Warren, Rick. *The Purpose Driven Life: What on Earth Am I Here For?* Grand Rapids, MI: Zondervan, 2012.

Xu, Jessica, and Helena Cooper Thomas. "How Can Leaders Achieve High Employee Engagement?" *Leadership & Organization Development Journal 32*, no. 4 (2011): 399–416. doi:10.1108/01437731111134661

Ziglar, Zig, and Tom Ziglar. *Born to Win: Find Your Success Code*. Ziglar Inc., 2014.